C000212206

Winner Or Loser –
My Choice

Dear Paul

Go for your dreams + never give up!

Love Tom

Winner Or Loser –
My Choice

By

Pam Hanson

Date of Publication: November 2002
Reprinted: April 2004

Published by:
Free As A Bird Publishing
PO Box 108
Stockport
SK6 8WX

Printed by:
ProPrint
Riverside Cottage
Great North Road
Stibbington
Peterborough PE8 6LR

ISBN:0-9543670-0-6

ABOUT THE AUTHOR

Pam is happily married to Ian and they live in High Lane in Stockport. She has spent much of the past twenty years bringing up their four children.

Pam has been writing for some time but has only recently considered herself to be a writer. She feels that her writing gives her a purpose – she has got something inside her that has got to come out – and is constantly amazed by the ideas that come up.

ACKNOWLEDGEMENTS

I would like to thank all those who have helped and encouraged me in all I am doing. I have thanked people individually in the text of my book but if I have forgotten anyone, please forgive me.

My brother's comment:
'A fascinating study in self-analysis'

Filled with extraordinary and sometimes unbelievable incidents, the writer's own life has inspired her to produce a text replete with the philosophical musings her experiences have summoned forth.

Her proposition is reminiscent of Ortega y Gasset's reflections on Don Quixote, that life is an act of will, that this human spirit will overcome all challenges provided only that we believe in ourselves and our own manifest destiny.

Michael Anderson

MAPS Manager

"In 'Winner Or Loser – My Choice' Pam Hanson takes the reader through incidents in her life in a kaleidoscopic way – one story sparks another, crisscrossing time and significance. Her style is engaging and warm. From beginning to end, her belief in the resilience of the human spirit shines through."

Jacqui Wood

Programme Co-ordinator, MAPS

If anyone would like to give Pam any feedback about her book contact her on: pamhanson20@hotmail.com or Free as a Bird Publishing PO Box 108, Stockport SK6 8WX. She would be very pleased to hear from you.

CHAPTER 1

Experiences and Growth

I have thought about writing my story for years, but I always felt that I never had the time. Then one night everyone had disappeared upstairs to watch 'the footy', so as I felt like a bit of company, I followed. I am not a real fan of the fine art of kicking a ball about. It doesn't do a lot for me; so I got to thinking about what I could do when everyone is upstairs 'goggling' the box. In fact if I organise the time I have sensibly, I will always be able to do what I really want to do. I know from experience that if I just write when I feel like it, time will pass and I'll never get round to it. I have already been working on my story for a number of months and I am beginning to get a feeling of urgency that will not let me stop. I realise that I will have to make a commitment to write every day and put a deadline on when it is to be finished. If a date is not put on a goal it is only a wish that shows no real commitment. I will have to make a timetable out and stick to it.

I want to be able to help others gain the self-knowledge that I have found so helpful in my life. That doesn't mean to say I have arrived, as the more I learn about myself the less I seem to know. The more excited I feel about what potential there is within me or in fact what potential there is within every one of us.

This got me thinking how things have changed and how much knowledge I have been taught by circumstances; how much quicker I would have learnt if I had had an open mind and been willing to change my opinions without so much of a fight. I think I could have been called dogmatic, domineering and rather forcefully direct, not willing to suffer fools gladly!

I may be wrong, I often am, but I believe the way of change is a long process. I couldn't grow unless I wanted to be different and I was quite happy with myself as I was. Until I realised I might have a better chance of getting what I wanted, if I allowed others to disagree with me with an acceptance of their point of view. Humility had to be the order of the day and a willingness to learn from other people's opinions and knowledge. My belief that I was always right had to be relinquished. It would be better for me and it would certainly benefit other people!

I began to think back to how I felt as a child – contained and controlled – probably because my dad, who was a headmaster, had to be obeyed with no argument. My mum told me I always used to reject the hugs I needed. I remembered the lack of physical contact as something that was never offered. It really shows how a child's perception can be so distorted, not willing to take responsibility for my own actions but apportioning the blame to another.

Being a rebel at heart and knowing I couldn't get away with anything with my dad, I think I took it out on my mum as she was a much more easy-going person. I felt out of control and utterly helpless, not being able to have my own way and feeling very resentful about it. I had not learned that that is life and it's like that for everyone. I felt it was only me and that everyone else was getting what they wanted with no problem. Many a time, I have been told I was a little terror, although I didn't think so. Wrapped up in my own little world and feelings, I forgot about everybody else. A little self-centred maybe! I think I needed some very sharp edges being rubbed off me – <u>a diamond in the rough</u>! I believe we all are – if we could all know that, there would be a lot less defensive, touchy people in this world with maybe not so much road rage, and people demanding their rights to the detriment of others. A little bit of self-respect can do a world of good for one's confidence.

My father scared me, a keen disciplinarian – HE WAS RIGHT – it was like living with a volcano; likely to erupt at any time. My poor mum who, she said, loved to have discussions with her father when she was younger found it very difficult to live in such a dictatorial household.

She was an only one and although she talked a lot about her dad she hardly ever mentioned her mum. I can just about remember my grandfather. He used to stand in front of the fire with his hands behind his back and he had one of those waxed handlebar moustaches that looked very impressive. My mum said he was a very positive gentleman and was always telling her that she could do anything she wanted to. I don't think mum ever got over his death, she missed him so much as she was always talking about his sayings and how much they helped her.

When mum's mother died, my grandfather married again and I think there was a lot of resentment there, as Aunty

Mary, as we called her, tried to take the place of my mum's mother. I remember mum saying that that would never be possible and she shouldn't have the audacity to think she could.

I was told that on the death of my grandfather I said that that would be easier for Aunty Mary now, as it would save her work. I think that was my child's way of blocking off the hurt. It is only recently that I have realised I must never have really grieved for him as it was too painful. This realisation has allowed the tears to flow after so many years and I remember him, rather than a dim distant figure of the past but with a warmth and gratitude for all he was and with much more clarity now. I remember the warmth and love in his eyes as he bent down to look at me. It made me feel so special and treasured.

This is something I have done all my life – to block off the hurt and not acknowledge it – because it is too painful; never to deal with it. That meant I put up barriers to protect myself and I never allowed people near me because I was frightened of being hurt again.

But somehow, between my dad and me I could sense there was a closeness. Feeling the depth of his love, the compassion deep within him that was not allowed to surface very often, as though he was afraid of being vulnerable.

When dad was a child he lost his father in the first world war; the only thing I know about my grandfather is that he used to play the mandolin. I think it hurt too much to talk about, as my dad never mentioned his father in my hearing. His mum was left on her own to bring up three young children.

My dad was the middle one between two girls; and his mum felt she could not cope with a rebellious young boy who had just lost his dad. She decided he needed a father figure, so he was sent to live with his grandfather and his second wife, who was known as Auntie Needham. My dad never mentioned what sort of life he had with them, but I had the feeling it was rather a strict environment. It will never be known as I cannot ask him because he died many years ago.

Years later my grandmother (dad's mum) sold her house to my mum and dad. Gran gran as she was called lived with each one of her children in turn until she died of cancer just before I was born. I was never aware of all this until my cousin shared about it when I told him I was writing my story. I would like to thank him for explaining things to me. It helps to know of dad's background and to realise the amount of hurt he must have had when he was only a youngster.

Dad's smile would show me the real man beneath the stern exterior. I could warm to him then! If we had been able to focus on the positive side of dad – being so direct, competitive and self-assured – we might have had a more peaceful household. If I can only concentrate on the positive side of people instead of always focusing on the negative it would make personal relationships so much easier and happier.

People are like flowers – we blossom and grow – when we receive a little bit of tender loving care. This helps us to believe in ourselves and do things we would never have believed possible before.

I sometimes ask myself what dad really thought about things. I wonder where he was coming from but I can only guess. I wonder whether the anger was his hurt coming out at being sent away from his mum, we will never know.

Dad

Warm smile
Thunder clouds
Over the horizon
What mood is he in?
Relaxed and happy
Black volcanic anger

Was he hurting?
Was he longing
To smash those barriers down
To reveal the love
Deep within his soul
That was aching to be set free

Habit locked him
In its grip
Fear of showing
His vulnerability.
Compassion
Interpreted as weakness
Never seeing
This is strength.

Writing about the past has made me see how it can shape us as people, especially if hurts have not been addressed and dealt with. It is right that we should not live in the past but if healing has not taken place we always will, as the hidden pain makes us behave in a less than desirable manner, and cause us even more hurt.

The subconscious is so powerful and whatever it is told is accepted as truth. If the continual information it is given is full of negative ideas such as 'I can't do this' or 'I am not worthy of that' then our actions reinforce our beliefs. When the expected result occurs we declare, 'See I told you so!' Our thoughts about ourselves are put into words and this is called self-talk, this is what influences our subconscious.

To change our self-talk is such a powerful tool when we want to become more confident and feel better about ourselves. It may seem a bizarre idea, but if our thoughts are monitored and noticed, then there is the possibility that we can change how we think by a definite act of will power, just changing what we say to ourselves. I know it is difficult to contemplate such action, i.e. to face up to those hurts, but from my own experience, believe me, it is worth it.

The only way that can be done is by having a burning desire to want to change, to want things to be better. There is an element of risk in all we do in life and the only reason we take that risk is that we believe the pay off (i.e. the result) will be worth it. The feeling of release and freedom has got to be experienced before the benefits can really be appreciated. I can feel myself relaxing and not feeling quite so scared about life. In fact the excitement about what can be in store is filling my heart with hope and anticipation. I know I am in control and it is up to me now.

Belief is another tool we can use to increase our quality of life. The longing for something that I find difficulty in believing I can have, is the start of a chain of thought processes that have changed my life. I would be in a wheelchair now if I had not believed I could reach the full recovery I anticipated. I expected it to happen which is another piece in the jigsaw of my growth. To expect the impossible is one step on the road to reach my desires, whatever they may be. To keep telling myself I can do it and that I can make it happen is the passport to my dreams. Never give up, <u>never</u> give up but just keep on doing whatever needs to be done, even though there doesn't seem to be any foreseeable results. <u>It will happen</u>. It will work for anyone if they want to try it but perseverance and consistency is the key to make it happen. Believe it and expect it and just keep on going. Success will follow.

When I moved to London I got a transfer from the Stationary Office in Oldham to Holborn Viaduct, where I was put into the publicity department with a very confident young lady as my boss, who was not very well endowed with patience. I can't really blame her as I would have tried the patience of a saint. My memory and concentration was still not at its best because of the brain damage I incurred from an accident I had had when I was twenty, so lots of mistakes were made.

When my boss went on holiday I was in charge and I took it on myself to submit an advert thinking I was showing my initiative, but when she returned and got the proof back she hit the roof and I was dispatched to the big man in charge – on the carpet again – the story of my life!

This man, called Charles, said that he was always sent the lame dogs and although I did not like being so called he was very sympathetic and made me feel there was hope for me yet. He suggested I should try the cataloguing department where I would be in charge of producing the Annual Catalogue of H.M.S.O. Publications – after of course I had had training.

I liked the idea of having that responsibility and I was pleasantly surprised at what the job entailed. I found I really enjoyed it. Helping the public on our enquiry line was also part of my duties. I enjoyed that as well, liking to be in contact with the public. The first year I was put in charge I was able to get it published earlier than any other year. When I was nearing my deadline I was given dispensation from dealing with the telephone enquiries.

That gave me quite a feeling of smugness as my colleagues were being bombarded by anxious members of the public; some important bill having been published that day. I could concentrate on getting the catalogue to press! This increased my powers of concentration no end and my immediate boss commented on my focus, another feather in my cap.

I was congratulated on this achievement by Charles. He was very pleased with my performance and he really made me feel good about myself. When I left the department he gave me a plant as a personal gift and years afterwards when it had been flourishing quite well it suddenly seemed to take sick and died. A long time afterwards I discovered Charles had died about that time.

I began to get very homesick so after about four years, Ian, my husband, managed to get a transfer up to the Stockport area; so when the sale of our maisonette finally came through, we had to move all our worldly goods to our new house up north. At the time I was expecting our first child, so because I was suffering very badly from morning sickness I was excused from helping with the removal. I just lay in bed feeling very sorry for myself, Ian's mum ministering to my every need!

I was so glad we had made the move as soon afterwards my dad had a heart attack so we were able to go over and see them. My parents had retired to North Wales so it would have been quite a trek from London. We went to visit him in hospital and all seemed to be going well, although he did have to go on a cholesterol-free diet and stop smoking. He seemed to be getting better and even had a gentle game of golf.

Quite a while afterwards he got pleurisy and we went to visit them for a few days. We were getting ready to go home when I had a feeling I should stay with mum. It saved having to pack all the baby things in the car as by then we had our eldest son Carl, who was only about six months. I waved Ian bye-bye and then went to talk to dad.

He seemed to be so at peace and he asked me to close a window for him, whispering that mum had been right as she had wanted to close it earlier. I did so, and then rubbed his back for him where the draught had caught him. I went to get Carl and mum came into the bedroom with me and we were standing chatting when mum had to go to the loo.

Just after she had gone my dad made a choking noise and seemed to slump forward. I rushed into the lounge, put Carl on the floor, checked everything was safe, and rushed back to dad's side. I started mouth-to-mouth resuscitation and when mum returned I told her to call the doctor. I knew he had gone but I had to keep on with the resuscitation until the doctor came and said there was no hope. What a shock, I was devastated!

My brother Peter was called and he took everything in hand rushing over from Oldham. I was in a state of shock and just felt numb. I stayed with mum till the funeral. It was only when I was shaking my cousin's hand, he had taken the service, that it suddenly came home to me and I burst into tears. It was an empty void with a tremendous feeling of loss. I could no longer ask him about his childhood and all the memories he must have had. I felt as though I had missed out on so much. Then followed a long period of mourning – a real uphill struggle.

This reminds me of another story where I thought I would have to do the same thing for my mum. This happened not long after dad's death. I had just had my second child, Keith, and mum came over to give me a hand.

We were talking in the lounge when she suddenly keeled over and I had visions of the same thing happening again, as I tried to revive her. Thinking I might have to resuscitate her, I tried to get her flat on the floor as she had fallen on the sofa. This was not a good idea as I succeeded in banging her head and causing a very nasty bruise. She was very cross with me when she recovered as it was really painful.

She slowly came round despite my bungled attempts at tender loving care and I helped her up to her bed where she rested until I could get a doctor to her. He was rather concerned as at first she did not respond to treatment but gradually she started to come round. I was feeling rather scared as Ian was away and I felt dreadfully alone. Mum was really upset as she kept bemoaning the fact that she was supposed to be helping not passing out on me!

She was fine by the time that Ian came home except for a rather sore head that she wouldn't let me forget about! After that experience she became frightened and never came again which was such a shame as we really enjoyed her staying with us. I understand how she must have felt but it is so sad when negative experiences in the past are allowed to rule the rest of our lives. Never daring to venture out to do something that didn't work out last time, for no other reason than the past. Maybe even trying it a different way does not come into the equation, as fear has taken control and it becomes a habit not to try something new. The thought that it may have a positive outcome is overridden by the belief that nothing will ever change. It becomes a self-fulfilling prophesy as nothing is even attempted, so of course everything stays the same and the comfort zone is kept intact with no scary deviation from the norm.

Another thought – exciting ideas are never put into effect because of the fear of failure or even a fear of success. So normally, people hold back the action that could possibly make their dreams come true. A person who wants to step out of the average mould could risk to do what is needed and be nearer to reach their full potential.

Through these experiences I have become much stronger as whatever happens I have always managed to cope. This gives me more confidence in myself and reinforces my belief that I will never be given more than I can cope with. Every challenge I am asked to face always seems to stretch me just a little bit further than I want to go. This enables me to learn new lessons; but I have to be willing to let go of my old way of thinking. I find this is exciting as then anything that begins to feel uncomfortable may well be a further step forward in my growth. I am happy with who I am now, but I always know that there are more mountains to scale, more growing to accomplish. I can be even more at peace, content and happy to be the person I have become, but to be aware that I have never finished my journey to fulfilment, until it is time for me to go home and meet my God.

I seem to spend parts of my life in a numb state where I go into a sort of limbo. I wander around in a lost trance not knowing what to do but just walking around on automatic pilot, getting done the essentials; no real sparkle in my eyes. I think sometimes we have to shut down to survive. When my emotions are in such a turmoil a nervous breakdown is on the horizon, having to switch off whilst healing is in progress.

Then after a period I am ready to face life again with all its ups and downs. Then off I go until the next time! I am not saying it is all doom and gloom, as there are so many things to be thankful for – the beauty of the world we live in and the kindness of ordinary everyday people. The news tends to focus on all the negative events in the world but there are plenty of good things happening. Occasionally the media open their eyes and we are delighted with some good news that they allow through their positive filter.

CHAPTER 2

Love

It was nice and cosy, warm and comfortable. This is the life, I thought! Then I felt a sort of pushing and I had a premonition of doom, a rather uncomfortable uncanny feeling – I resisted. It would not go away. I was being expelled from my safe happy haven. I did not want to leave but I had no say in the matter.

I began to feel frightened until it turned into a pure naked terror of the unknown. I felt myself pushed along a dark passage engulfed by a tide of dark liquid. I could not breathe for what seemed like an eternity. Then I was struck with a dazzling powerful light that hurt my eyes; I exploded into the world screaming my displeasure at being so callously disturbed.

No comfort and loving tender care for me. Just put under a blanket and torn away from the only safe place I had ever known. My mother was not even allowed to hold me. I did not like that and I let people know – and how! I filled my lungs with air and let rip. I was not going to take this quietly!

I have begun to realise this might have been the reason I was so insecure and frightened as a child. My subconscious might even have harboured resentment against my mum, for not being there when I needed her, even though she had no say in the matter. The workings of a child's mind has no rhyme or reason and logic does not come into it, especially with me as logic is not one of my strong points.

You would think that when I reached maturity I would see the folly of that resentment, but as it was hidden deep in my subconscious, I had no way of knowing from where those bad feelings were coming. Of course all the blame was put on my mum. Maybe deep hurts are only healed if they are acknowledged and dealt with, which means that some rather painful digging has to be done in the subconscious. The only way that can be achieved is if I am ready to take that risk.

Not being very good at accepting responsibility for my feelings or actions, it was easier to blame mum, as that meant I had no need to do anything. I could just relax and wait for her to change. That is a very naïve and self-centred attitude as that is assuming that I am always in the right and no-one could possibly disagree with me. Can I detect a little duplication of my dad do you think?

It is reasonable to assume I would have learnt from his mistakes but not Pamela; he might have been wrong but not me! I have found by experience that people will only change if they really want to and know they need to for their own good, but even then the fear of change can sometimes sabotage their good intentions.

Love

What a mystery!
How powerful
Flows that
Unknown entity
Of Ethereal existence

Where does it come from?
Within my soul
Bubbling
In a deep reservoir
Of untapped potential.

Wanting to overflow
Flooding
The hurting wounded
Of life casualties

Lower the floodgates
Of my insecurities
Bring those barriers down
Of my painful past.

Breaking free
To be the person I was meant to be.

Somebody else was feeling just as frustrated. I heard a loud voice close to me and felt the blanket being lifted and a sharp slap was administered to my bare leg. The shock made me gasp and that terror seemed to grip me again, seeming to paralyse me. My noise abated until I started sobbing in absolute despair. I then felt myself lifted up and held close and rocked to and fro until absolutely exhausted with my ordeal I fell asleep.

The power of love is something that never ceases to amaze me. It never pushes, never screams for attention but is there waiting, for when the hurting one is ready to receive it. It is such a healing quality and can defuse so many situations. If there is anger and hurt present, acceptance of that person's feelings and attitudes, which is what love means, is healing and soothing for someone experiencing deep trauma.

To be heard in this busy and stressed world is unusual. Taking the time to listen and let people blow off steam usually helps them to rid themselves of the pressure that has probably been building up for quite a period of time. The effect of some tender loving care is remarkable, as a grumpy touchy individual can be transformed into a warm loving person, who opens up like the tightly closed bud of a carnation, when the time for maturity has arrived.

Wonderful Profusion

Blooms of joyous pinks, white and reds
Exploding from the vase,
Interspersed with the green
Of their foliage,
Spreading their joyous
Love of life
As the closed buds
Unfold to reveal their hidden glory.

Lifting their petals
In adoration
Of their maker
As they take in
The life-giving water.

Showing us mortals
How to appreciate
What we have
With no regret

Of yesterday,
With no fear
Of the future.
Living
For the now
And glorying in it.

I woke up and began to feel frightened – of what I did not know. I began to cry as that was the only way I knew of expressing my feelings. I was picked up and given food. Whilst I was held, I felt secure and loved, I was happy. As soon as I was put down I lost the feeling of security that being held gave me; my fear returned and I let everyone know about it. Then I felt a gentle rocking – I felt soothed again – feeling safe and happy.

Why I was affected by the birth experience that everyone has to go through, is a mystery for me. This is the only way I can account for my memories of the past. I could well be wrong but if it satisfies me, it doesn't matter what others may think as they are not the ones dealing with my traumas. I had to find an explanation for my resentment as a child because of the person I am. It feels right now but if at a later date I change my mind and find another way of looking at it, that is OK as everyone is allowed the freedom of a change of heart.

If everyone stays the same, what a boring world it would be. There would be no growth or moving on and the world would pass away without a ripple in sight. Maybe you do not agree but everyone is different, I am glad to say.

A baby is so vulnerable and helpless. It's a little person having its own feelings with only one way to express its anxiety and fear. I was always frightened of something when I was a child therefore I could never relax and be the real me. It was as though I was always looking over my shoulder in case whatever I was afraid of manifested itself – never being able to put a name to it. I wouldn't even accept the hugs I needed. I just distanced myself from everyone. It's strange how fear can rule your life but it took me a long time to begin to work things out. It is this journey I am sharing with you hoping it will help others to journey on to their full potential.

I never really got on with my mum when I was growing up. I always seemed to shut her out. I know she felt hurt but it is only recently I have begun to see what was happening. I did not even realise that it was me that was the problem but blamed my mum for the bad feelings I had. Everything she did was interpreted as a slight against me so it was not surprising that there was friction between us, and that I could find no good in her.

My cousin's memories of her have made me see my mum in a different light. He said that when he married, his wife really appreciated how my mum made her feel welcome, as my mother realised that admittance into a close knit family was quite a daunting undertaking, especially as she had already been through that herself. With her being an only child to become part of the close family of my dad's must have been a great joy for her.

I remember the Christmas parties we used to have. They were renowned in our family for the good food that she used to make and the fun we used to have. Dad was in his element too as he was in charge of the party games we used to play. Blinds man buff where someone was blindfolded and had to catch one of the revellers as they ran round the one who was on. Screams of delight as a daring soul went a bit too close and paid for his bravado by being snatched and blindfolded.

There was pass the parcel and musical chairs and a very messy game involving a pile of flour with a chocolate perched on top. A knife was handed round to cut away the flour and when the sweet was dislodged the offending culprit had to pick it up with their teeth, their hands tied behind their back. Squeals of joy as the unfortunate one got covered in flour as the prize evaded their grasp.

All the fun was forgotten when normal life returned and I went back to feeling sorry for myself again without being able to see that I could enjoy life even though there were no parties on the horizon.

All the hurt seems to be healed now. I am so thankful for being able to see my mum as she really was. It is as though a veil has been lifted from my eyes and I can see clearly now. She died not so long ago at the age of eighty-nine and I am happy that we were able to relate to one another as a mother and daughter really should. We did seem to be getting closer as we both got older and I was beginning to see things from her prospective, - walking in her shoes. I was able to spend time with her, that is very special for me. I did write a poem for her that I read at her funeral:

Mum

Missing you.
No crooked smile
To warm my heart.
No frail form
To wonder at.
No fighting spirit
That would never give in.
No stubborn will
That would never sway.
Time willingly given
To be at your side.
Seconds ticking away
Towards your final goodbye,
When you are released
To make your final journey
Home.

No pain, no sorrow –
Only peace and joy.
Questions answered.
So simple
That we on earth
Can never see.

You know true happiness now.

Watching over us
With your love
That will never fade.
Accept our gratitude
And farewell until we meet again.

Whenever I read this poem, tears flow as grief takes over. I remember how encouraging she was with any of our new ventures. The belief she had in me was a real blessing that I never felt as a child.

Unforgiveness is something I have struggled with all my life. It eats away within me making me more and more bitter, all bound up in my own little world, allowing no light to enter to relieve my pain. When I can release the hurt, and forgiveness finally is allowed to seep into my soul, it's like a burden being lifted off my shoulders, joy wells up within me and I suddenly realise that I have nothing to forgive.

I begin to see things from the forgiven person's perspective. It feels as though God's love fills my being as I realise I have been forgiven for so much that I have no right to be unforgiving of others.

That is one advantage of getting older – gaining wisdom from the books I have read and learning from the things I have done. Success is only achieved by dint of persistence and perseverance.

Failure becomes success by never giving up, always being focussed on what is wanted and acting as though it is reality before actions make it happen. Despite the storm clouds ahead do not be deterred, keep on going a step at a time; a journey of a thousand miles begins with a single step.

As time has passed I feel as though I have mellowed. I have begun to understand what compassion means. How much more pleasant life is to approach a situation with peace and love in my heart rather than barriers up and guns blazing.

There is nothing wrong in disagreeing with someone; that happens, it's life. How boring it would be if we all thought the same. What I have begun to see are the many colours of other ideas making life so much more exciting, a kaleidoscope of vibrant hues. Thinking of others can give me a new way of looking at things, can even make me grow and reach higher realms. Reaching for the stars can involve listening to others to broaden my own limited vision.

I have been so closed and blinkered, not able to see points of view different to mine, limiting my own perspective by not looking outside my own experience.

The realisation of something so basic gives me that wonderful feeling of soaring into a bright blue summer's sky like an eagle. It gives me such a feeling of freedom and power over my own destiny. All I have to do is act on the ideas I have, putting behind me all my fears and inhibitions and just go for it.

CHAPTER 3

Teenager

Maths, I thought – who cares how many bricks he builds in his stupid wall anyhow. – I have just got a mental block with numbers I decided; I had better ask dad. I explained the difficulty of not being able to understand how to do it. My father spent hours trying to explain it to me but I could not see it.

He finally gave up, saying that I was not trying. He had started shouting in anger and frustration at my stupidity. I had switched off; it was the only way I could cope with the terror that his shouting gave me. I felt so rejected and so hurt. I felt no good and no use to anyone.

I knew it was exasperating for dad but that did not help me as I had really tried despite what he thought. My fear of failing had blocked my ability to understand and I felt a real disappointment to him. My fear of not being the person my dad wanted me to be had defeated me, the terror I felt at not coming up to his expectations had made me retreat into insolence and bravado. I felt utter despair and retreated even further into myself.

Now I have found that fear is such a negative, terrifying emotion; it stops me from doing so much. It immobilises me so that I never reach my full potential. Those who have never failed have never done anything. Why not Feel the Fear and Do It Anyway? It is easy to say but whatever I fear usually never happens anyhow. Why waste precious time on it! I have only one life so why not use the time I have got productively and enjoy whatever I am doing – it really is my choice. There is no need regretting the past; that is over so I have decided to accept it and learn from it – when I remember!

My dad said he was going to the newsagents and asked me if I wanted to go. I felt a real thrill; so privileged as to be allowed to go with him. It was a really happy joyous feeling of being with someone I loved and I knew loved me. I felt as though I was walking on air, I was getting some attention that I was never allowed to ask for as he was always so busy.

When my dad was not working I was always told not to bother him as he needed to relax. As we got into the car I felt like a princess going on a great adventure. We did not need to talk; I just enjoyed being with him. We got there and parked and then he held my hand as we crossed the road.

As dad paid for the papers, I looked at the display of sweets with an envious eye. Then my dad asked me if I would like something and not needing a second invitation I shared what I would like – my special favourite.

He said to the man behind the counter, 'That's all she comes for!'

It felt like a bombshell had fallen on my fantasy world and I began to feel misjudged and rejected. He really thought that about me! I began to feel so angry that nobody seemed to be able to see good in me. I was always credited with negative motives. Could not anyone see the real me or was I really as bad as people painted?

It is really surprising how a chance comment from an adult can hurt an impressionable child who takes it on board, becoming part of them. Each negative word builds up a portfolio of hurtful phrases that are stored up in the subconscious, convincing the young person of their lack of worth as a human being.

I remember when Mark, my youngest son, came with me to a shop and I offered to buy him some sweets and of course he accepted. I said to the man behind the counter, 'That's all he comes for.' His look of hurt surprise really said it all. There was an element of defiance there as well so that was a healthy way of reacting to my negative comment.

Thank goodness he was not following in my footsteps of hurt rejection. Children are so resilient today, which is a relief for me as my mistakes are so many. I am surprised that mine have grown up to be so well adjusted young people.

As my dad got older he seemed to me to mellow. He never talked much but we enjoyed each other's company and seemed to get closer. My mum and I seemed to get on better too. Maybe it was me getting older, having the responsibility of bringing four children up, their dad not being around a lot, that made me a bit more accepting of others.

My memories of childhood always seem to be so negative. I know there were good times as my parents really loved me. There were those parties I mentioned earlier and the times we used to go searching for wild flowers in the Derbyshire dales. We also used to have some lovely holidays.

We found a farm in South Wales where the farmer let out a cottage where we self catered. There was a cat there that used to sit up and beg for titbits so when we got back home we taught our cat to do the same. As he was a stray ginger tom, that was easy to do, as food was his most important aim in life. He would do anything for that, so sitting up on his back legs was no problem.

Once when we were at the farm it was haymaking time so we all joined in with a will and had a great time. They also kept cows and in those days they used to milk them all by hand.

Imagine my excitement when they said they would teach me how. They were very impressed when the cow I was milking stood there docilely when she could have just walked away, as they had forgotten to tie her up.

The cows all had their own names and characters and it was fascinating to get to know them. They are very lovable creatures with their big soft eyes and leisurely walk. I sometimes think we could learn from them, maybe taking our time a little more and not rushing at breakneck speed at everything we do.

I am not advocating that we should copy them all the time, as chewing the cud all day is not my idea of enjoyment – not a lot would get done. The point I am making is that we all need to smell the roses sometimes (i.e. take a little time for ourselves to do something we enjoy) but we cannot spend all our time doing that, otherwise there would be no growth and life would be totally boring – for me anyway! I know some people would disagree with me but it takes all sorts to make a world and everyone is different.

There would be no feeling of achievement and fulfilment for a job well done, if everyone sat around chewing their cud all day. With me being an action person that would be purgatory for me! There are arguments for both sides!

When I was a teenager my mum was left some money by an aunt who we used to go and see sometimes. She decided to invest that money by buying a bungalow in Wales as she was very fond of that country.

When she was a child she was sent there for her health as she had a bad chest and ended up with bronchiectasis, the air being so much cleaner in that part of the world. She stayed with some relatives and really enjoyed her time there. The doctor would not let her go to school because she had to spend as much time as possible in the fresh air. Mum used to talk about that sometimes and her love of Rhyl stemmed from that time. I think she said she used to take their dog for walks and the bracing air really did her a lot of good.

That meant all our holidays were spent there. My mum found a bungalow in a small place called Rhuddlan, near to Rhyl, and we spent all spare weekends there. The pace of life was much slower and it was just right for mum and dad although after the first initial excitement and novelty I began to get rather bored.

Looking for entertainment I soon got talking to the men who were working on the building site. The son of the owner of the building company asked me out but all he wanted was to go up quiet secluded lanes and indulge in a bit of cuddling. He did not get very far but he had the cheek to say that he thought I would prefer it that way. Still being a bit shy I did not enlighten him on the subject although I was a bit peeved as I was really out for a good time. I would not have been averse to a night on the town!

It was not to be. After a few dates he called it a day and said it would never work because it never had before. I didn't really know what he meant but he would not elucidate. I was rather upset; I had got to really like him as well as my pride being hurt. After he faded away I began to lose interest in going to Wales as there was nothing to do for a teenager. When I was old enough I persuaded my mum and dad to let me stay at home as Peter, my brother felt the same way as me, and didn't often go, so I would not be on my own.

Teenager Blues

Why is everyone against me?

Why does no one see my point of view?

No one listens

No one cares

Controlled, contained

Feeling like a caged

Majestic eagle,

Aching for its freedom

Resentment fills my soul

A canker

That eats away

My self esteem

That gives me no rest!

A dark cloud

Of my own making

Centre of the universe

Focused on me

Inspiration dawns.

Love and compassion for others

- Peace at last!

It was as though I thought I did not deserve to be happy because of my lack of self esteem. I was always sabotaging the good things that happened to me, to reinforce my own beliefs, blaming circumstances for my bad luck, not realising it was me that was making it happen.

Always saying I couldn't do things, always expecting the worst, making me a prophet of doom and of course I proved myself right. I am learning that the more I think positive thoughts the better life becomes, not because this makes me immune to unfortunate circumstances but it gives me a better attitude to life so that I am able to cope better with the small disasters that life throws at me.

I used to think that it was only me that had to go through these traumas as though I was the only one on this earth with problems. Life experience has taught me otherwise especially when you hear of all the sad stories in the papers. It has really made me aware of all the good things in my life giving me the wonderful gift of gratitude for the many gifts I have been given. Not least just being alive and having all my senses!

I remember one time at Youth Club two girls complimented me on my tan. Instead of accepting the compliment and continuing the conversation I went into a long discourse on how long I had to spend in the sun to achieve it. They lost interest and wandered away. I was too abrupt and full of myself in an attempt to hide my shyness and inferiority complex.

I had to learn that we have two ears and one mouth; we should use them in that proportion if we want to make friends. People are more interested in themselves. Everyone is like that.

Why do you think I am writing this book? As well as hoping to help others it is very good for my own ego! I think I needed to sort my own thoughts out and look back and see what I had learnt from my past experiences. Maybe to remind myself of the gems of knowledge that I had stored away in my subconscious, burying it there as using those experiences meant I had to move out of my comfort zone, (the familiar place, where I feel safe maybe but not happy,) – perhaps even to grow a bit which can be rather painful at times.

I find that I really have to force myself to start changing my way of thinking as it is so much more comfortable to stay where I am. That would ensure I would get stuck in a rut and not move on. I have a good old pity party moaning about life, thinking that I can't do anything about it because of the lot life has dealt me; not realising that those misfortunes that knocked me flat might well be opportunity in disguise.

Whenever I have had to change direction because of disastrous circumstances I have always found with hindsight that it was the best thing that could have happened to me.

CHAPTER 4

Flying like a bird

These thoughts take me back to when I was twenty –
flying through the air like a bird – but this bird had no
wings. After three hundred and fifty feet there was a very
heavy landing, resulting in the Glencoe Mountain Rescue
being called out to get me off the mountain. After three
weeks in a coma my family and boyfriend got ready to
leave as the doctors said it was unusual for anybody to
come round after so long.

A final visit by my dad to the intensive care unit changed
everything. Gazing through the outside window at me I
responded by waving to him!

Gradually I became more aware of my surroundings.
Having to start from scratch as I was as helpless as a
baby. This taught me patience and the ability not only to
accept my limitations but also to work towards the
change I believed would happen. I wasn't going to spend
the rest of my days in a wheelchair – I had the whole of
my life ahead of me and life was for living!

When I was in hospital I was as brown as a berry, as the
weather had been glorious for the time we had been on
holiday in Scotland, and the nurses good naturedly teased
me about having such a lovely tan.

I had a really good appetite – after not eating properly for
three weeks I suppose it isn't really surprising – breakfast
was the highlight of my day as I developed a real love for
porridge! The Scottish have a real way of making it and

with extra brown sugar and piping hot it was my idea of bliss.

I had to be fed at first but as that is not a very pleasant experience I soon began to manage a spoon by myself, making one more step along the road to recovery. Every little stride is a move in the right direction. I remember the occupational therapist came to teach me how to dress myself. I had great fun with trying to put my tights on, until she showed me how to roll each leg up separately, popping my toes in to make it easy to pull the rest up.

That was over thirty years ago. How time flies! Looking back at the sequence of events that put me in hospital I remember the struggle I had of getting up that rock face. The feeling that I would never overcome those obstacles – the hard rock that was so unyielding – of being coaxed up by Dave, the leader who had gone before me.

He was sitting belayed above me, giving me tips of where the holds were and how to use the leverage of my own weight to get over the overhang. Ian and Jim were belayed on another rope behind us watching our progress. It had been decided that I should climb with the most experienced as I was the beginner in the party.

I remember the smell of the grass as I started clambering up the smooth green slope that led to the ledge where Dave was waiting; of relaxing and thinking, 'I've done it.' That was the mistake. I lost concentration and slipped, feeling my legs losing purchase and sliding down and over the rocks I had just laboriously climbed.

The raw terror and then having the sensation of flying through the air that gave me a pleasure that made me forget the fear – and then oblivion.

The belay should have held as Dave had tied on with three belays which should have been enough with most climbs – but not with this one – as they all pinged out one after another. This meant that he was pulled after me and landed a few feet below me. He didn't have a helmet on but his only injuries were a broken arm and bad back. How he escaped head injury we just do not know. We lost touch following meeting up with him for a drink after I had left hospital. What became of him afterwards I just don't know – I often wonder!

Ian said that he and Jim watched with horror as I made the unscheduled descent. It is due to them that I am alive today. They both abseiled down to where I lay. Examining me they found I was unconscious so Jim rushed down the mountain to alert the rescue team. Ian stayed with me to make sure I fell no further.

I would like to thank them publicly for saving my life due to the efficient way they got the rescue team to me. The Glencoe Mountain Rescue Team did a wonderful job of getting me to Fort William Hospital and I would like to thank them also for their life saving work.

Life is exciting to me now. I soar like a bird when everything is fantastic and then something happens that tries to push me off course. As I have grown older taking knocks has become less traumatic with the length of time wallowing in self-pity becoming shorter!

I have come to realise that feeling sorry for myself saps me of my potential, putting up barriers that stop me from moving on. I have to venture out of my comfort zone and start looking ahead with confidence, secure in the knowledge that all I have to do is to go ever upwards and onwards.

To me success does not mean material wealth but a deep joy within me of spiritual well-being; of being happy with my lot and with who I am, accepting my faults and glorifying in my strengths. Always looking to forge forward searching for better things but not being devastated if it is not to be.

Flying like a bird

Contained and controlled

Prison

In a cage

Wings clipped

Miracle of growth

Freedom

Joy

Transformation

Breaking free

Fulfilment

Of becoming

The person I am meant to be.

No inhibitions

Just peace

As my love

Blossoms forth

And gives of itself

To share with others

The insights of my soul

It all sounds so simple as though I came to these conclusions without any pain. It took a lot of set-backs and loads of insight – I have got a long way to go yet but at least I know where I am going! I know I am here on this earth to write, and now I have found my vocation. Part of my mission is to tell what I have learnt from my experiences in life, to give everyone I meet a smile and to share my joy of living, hoping to make a difference by giving people a little bit of hope.

My faith also had a lot to do with my growth as the knowledge that I was a walking miracle made me feel my God must have something very special for me to do. The knowledge that someone is always there with me gives me a confidence that whatever life throws at me I will come through it and out the other side a better person. Even though I get scared sometimes I know I will never be asked to go through more than I can cope with, somehow there is always something positive coming out of it all.

I always remember being a very lonely child and always being bored and asking my mum, 'What can I do?' After giving me a few suggestions, which I duly rejected she gave up and had to get on with her jobs.

I always seemed to feel empty inside and always relied on outside influences to give me stimulus to do something. It was as though I had no interest or opinions outside myself; that I lived in a cocoon of my own making, insulated from other people's ideas and thoughts, frightened of what they may think about me. Not allowing anyone near to penetrate that prickly outer shell I had erected round myself, guarding against anyone becoming too important to me as there would always be the risk of losing them. Always frightened of being hurt, never realising that risk is part of life, the enjoyment and fun far outweighing the fear that tries to stop me.

I began to retreat into books and became a real bookworm living in a fantasy world, going through someone else's adventures and making them my own. I was very shy and unsure of myself so that my lack of self-confidence made me think no one would be interested in what I had to say. When some interest was shown I froze with fear with no words coming out and I was left with my mouth open looking like a goldfish!

When I was in my teens I remember that I did have a friend who went to my dad's school. We were always out together and got on really well. Then apparently she was caught stealing and she tried to talk to me about it. My self-righteous indignation erected my barriers and the poor girl was left feeling rejected and misjudged.

That was the end of a friendship that had possibilities. When I think about it now I want to curl up in a ball and bury myself in a deep hole never to be seen again! What a friend I turned out to be! I sabotaged any hope of cementing our relationship and becoming closer, by refusing to let her share what had really happened and how she had succumbed to the temptation. Compassion was not my strong point, but as time has gone on, gradually beginning to understand what a blessing it can be to allow others to open up; to have the privilege to listen and see them blossom under the shower of tender loving care.

CHAPTER 5

Education!

The only school I can remember anything of is the grammar school near my home. My mum and dad sent me to the prep school where I was quite happy. I really got into the flower competition that they had every year. It entailed collecting wild flowers and labelling them with their name both Latin and English. These days it would not be allowed but in my day it was acceptable. I was taken out to the Derbyshire Dales to search for new species that I found very exciting. A record was kept of all the ones I had collected and there was a prize for the one who had collected the most. I don't think I ever won the first prize but it was the competition I liked.

I had to take an entrance exam at the end of my second year and much to my disappointment I failed. This meant I had to stay down a year and take it again. Whilst I was talking to the girls who were going up to the 'Big School' they made some derogatory statement about one of the girls with whom I was staying down. I didn't defend her as I used to go along with what everyone said. She overheard and she would never forgive me even though I apologised to her. Another lesson, I can never take any actions or words back, so always think before I act or speak. I didn't learn that lesson straight away as I still kept opening my mouth and putting my foot straight in it!

I never really got to know any of the girls there as I always went home for dinner. If I had stayed for lunch, which I refused point blank to do, I might have had some of the sharp corners knocked off me sooner. When one of the girls told me how good the meals were I did change my mind but by that time mum said it was too late and I would have to wait till next term. By then I forgot to remind her, so then it became a habit and I never did anything about it.

It seemed to me I was surrounded by clever confident girls which made me feel inadequate until I thought to myself, 'Why should they have all the fun,' and started coming out of my shell and being the real me! Even so the shy timid me was always ready to surface if I had too many set-backs; as I am growing older I find it much easier to be the real me – much to the chagrin of my family – as I know I can be a bit overpowering at times!

Like most people my life seems to progress in a series of peaks and troughs. I wasn't particularly inspired with school life as I felt that those who excelled in anything were applauded but those who just jogged along weren't given any encouragement but just left to their own devices.

When it was time to take my GCEs all my teachers said I couldn't possibly get seven subjects, but my headmistress, who knew my dad, insisted I could. I decided to prove her right and set to with a will to come up to her expectations.

The boy I was going out with at the time was doing his 'A' levels so he said we would have to finish until after the exams. I was a bit peeved about that but it really was the best thing that could have happened to me as I had nothing else to do except study for my 'O's.

Tell me I can't do something and it's like a red rag to a bull and I just go ahead and do it! The results came out and a postcard came through the door with 'Congratulations' written in the headmistress's own handwriting. Recognition at last! Basking in approval didn't last long.

I had decided I wanted to go to physiotherapy college, but I had to be eighteen. I got in at Sheffield as that college didn't need 'A' levels. Much to everyone's disapproval I decided to stay at school for another year doing an 'A' level course but never taking an exam. Although my mum maintained it was a waste, I have come to the conclusion that it was all in the scheme of things.

Making me grow, learning not to waste precious time and appreciating how life can be so full and exciting. Time is such a wonderful gift that we don't really appreciate. We just take it for granted. It is the one thing that is free and we can never get it back. The knowledge that I have only a certain amount of time on this earth makes me live each day as though it is my last. Not meaning to be morbid but being truthful.

If I am not careful I so easily forget and wish my life away especially if there is something I am looking forward to in the future. It's what you make of it – enjoying what you have and focusing on the good things. That's what I know now, but then I was only seventeen. I had a lot to go through before the realisation dawned that I couldn't blame others for my challenges. It was up to me to accept them and overcome them, and learn from the many mistakes I make. I've discovered that it doesn't help me to focus on what I haven't got as this pulls me down into depression. As I don't like that feeling I have decided that it is not a good idea so I am learning not to do that now – sometimes!

Finally my dreams came true and I was off to Sheffield, I was really looking forward to leaving home but as soon as I was out in the big wide world, on my own, I got scared and became really homesick. I was used to all my decisions being made for me. I wasn't ready for the freedom. I had no organisation skills and was like a fish out of water and felt totally lost. I wasn't mature enough to learn from the experience. I just foundered and made a mess of my first exams. I loved the practical work in the hospitals but hated the theory – which you need before you can do the job! I kept on focusing on what I could not do instead of buckling down and getting on with what had to be done. I panicked so I did not learn a thing.

It seems to me that panic is a terrifying fear that immobilises me and makes me unable to think straight or make sense of the most mundane of actions. Realising this gives me a clue of how I can deal with panic – if I can use the power of logic, and rationalise my fears to persuade myself of the truth that fear is <u>False Evidence Appearing Real</u> which could well give me the control of panic for which I am searching. This may well seem obvious to more logical souls but to me it is a revelation!

Panic

Out of control
What can I do
Mind blank with fear
Terror filling my heart
Spiralling down
Into the black abyss
Of despair
STOP

Glimmer of hope
In that black pit
Gain control
By grasping
The window of opportunity
That is always
Waiting
For brave souls
Who dare

I never made any real friends and thought something was wrong with them. I did not ask myself why this was happening again. I suppose you could have called me a little arrogant at times. I could not see the obvious because of course I was right – still duplicating my dad, perhaps?

My mum and dad helped me to find somewhere to live in Sheffield, as there were no halls of residence at the college. At first I stayed at Y.W.C.A with a lot of other girls where meals were provided and certain rules that had to be kept. There always seemed to be arguments at the dinner table.

One girl, who I rather liked and could relate to, was very fastidious and complained about butter in the jam. I did not like it either but I was too shy to agree with her. Voices were raised and the atmosphere could be cut with a knife! If I had made friends with that girl we might have been good buddies but I just kept my mouth shut and agreed with everybody. I was so unsure of myself I was really a bit of a quiet mouse when I had to face the big wide world.

I then lived in a bed-sit with an alcove containing a hob where I could make my meals. It wasn't luxury but it was my own pad where I could do what I liked. I thought I would love it but I found it very lonely, as I was not one for my own company. There were other people staying in the same house but I didn't see much of them. One older lady though let me borrow her room, whilst she was away, for Ian, when he came to stay for the weekend.

We used to go to a nightclub, I really enjoyed the noise and the dancing and the cabaret acts, although I remember one being a bit blue which we didn't appreciate. Everyone else was roaring for more. We thought it wasn't really our scene so Ian decided not to go again, although I felt a little bit peeved about not being consulted. I don't think he liked the noise that I thrived on. Opposites attract!

Me being me, I was asked out by another lad. He insisted on taking me out even though I told him I was already going out with someone. I never refuse a free meal and entertainment so he did the honours. He was tall and thin and very self-confident and his attitude that he was a girl's dream come true really annoyed me. He didn't seem to notice and seem to thrive on the brush-offs I kept giving him. When I was going home for Christmas I told him I didn't want to see him again as my boyfriend and me were getting serious. He gave me his phone number and said I would be back, that made sure I made a point of losing his number never to be seen again!

One Christmas we had a party – it was when I had just started going out with Ian just before I went to college. I invited the boy who had finished with me because of his 'A' levels. Even though that had been good for me it had hurt my pride and it was my mum that suggested he should be asked. Ian brought his guitar so I spent all my time admiring his musical talents making it clear my affections had been captured by another! Now I feel a bit guilty about how I treated him. I could have been a bit more pleasant and still stayed friends but that was how I was, leaving a trail of broken relationships with no appreciation of others' feelings and wondering why they weren't very friendly if ever I saw them again.

I used to go to Church with my cousins when I was a teenager, and a young man there caught my eye but I did not get very far. He went to the Youth Club and afterwards a girl I had got friendly with invited us over to her house for a coffee. She knew I was keen and was trying to play cupid! We stayed quite late and stood chatting at the bottom of our road.

When I managed to drag myself away from him and was dreamily meandering back home, I was speedily brought back to reality by a car, driven by my dad, screeching to a halt by my side. An angry voice asked me what time I called this. My dad was really out of his mind with worry and I apologised profusely saying I had forgotten the time. Was I glad I hadn't stayed talking longer as my young man would certainly been regaled with some choice comments from my dad.

We did go out once but we were both so painfully shy that nothing came of it. There are so many occasions where a feeling of not being good enough completely sabotages any happy ending – don't get me wrong I know I am a very lucky lady having a man like Ian as my husband and I am certainly not complaining.

So many people never achieve their full potential because they think they are not good enough, all because of the negative feedback of childhood. Children are told so often that they can't do things, that they are stupid, that they can't expect a lot out of life and that they mustn't get their hopes up. Children then become parents and copy what was said to them. So the spiral goes on with each generation until one brave soul breaks the mould and starts thinking for themselves, changing from a negative mindset to a positive one. Giving their offspring the encouragement they need to reach their full potential. Everyone needs to have hope; that is what makes the world go round. If it does not work out then there is no need to give up, just try again, maybe in a different way and keep on going until the required effect is achieved.

Everyone is a unique person with their own gifts. There is no one else like you with both good and bad qualities. Concentrate on the excellent parts of you – everyone has some of those, whatever you think – and the nasty bits will become less important as the positive parts are focused upon.

If I am honest with myself I know what needs to be done about my less than good traits, but I have got to be willing to work on them. The first hurdle I have to overcome is to accept that there is a problem and then to find out what it is; that is to remove the blinkers I have habitually worn for over forty years.

For me I think I have to bring the barriers down that I must have erected so many years ago when my grandfather died, to protect myself from being hurt. The love I have within me has to be allowed to surface so that I can become the person I am meant to be, opening myself to others without the fear of rejection. This fear is responsible for so much lack of achievement in relationships.

Taking risks is part of life and those who run away from them stay where they are with no hope of moving forward. If it doesn't work out then start again with hope in your heart but never, never give up however many times you have to try. There are many self-help books that can give you examples of failing turning into success, never giving up until the goal is reached. Risk makes life an adventure, although a good self-image is helpful as there has to be a belief that whatever happens you will be able to cope. Maybe just risking can be the start of self-belief as you find you do cope with whatever occurs, whether good or bad!

Looking at problems as opportunities can take the fear away for me and give things a more exciting flavour so that fear goes out of the window. I can really enjoy my life with a spring in my step and hope welling up within me, I know nothing can stop me now!

CHAPTER 6

Marriage and Kids

All cares forgotten, I was off on a climbing holiday to Scotland, little knowing how it would change my life, with two young men – my boyfriend Ian, and his best friend Jim, who was also my ex. Strange set up! Jim had been going out with two girls at the same time, one being me, neither of us being aware of it. One time we were at the same party, and he managed to keep us both happy – a man of many talents – his friends who were in the know, were having hysterics watching his antics. He finally gave up the intrigue when he discovered he was double booked and begged Ian to take one off his hands. I was the lucky one and he turned up on my doorstep and the rest is history.

The great event arrived, my wedding day – 30th January 1971. I was walking on air. I was surprised I was so calm and confident. Everybody seemed to be rushing round demented but of course I didn't have to worry about anything except looking my best! I went to have my hair done and proudly told my hairdresser about my wedding dress that was velvet and had a hood with swans down round the edges. He was imagining real swans running round my face until he realised what I meant and we had quite a laugh about that as he was putting the finishing touches to my hair.

My mum and dad paid for all the wedding expenses, including my dress. Ian and I went into Manchester to look round the shops to get ideas; but when I saw this dream of a wedding dress I just had to have it, despite the cost. It was more than they wanted to pay so I hurriedly rang home from a call box (no mobiles in those days) and informed my mum I had found the one I wanted. She was a bit shocked with the price but said she would come and have a look at it. I used my powers of persuasion – it would be a winter wedding, would be warm and she wouldn't want her only daughter to get cold – so dreading what Dad would say she agreed with trepidation. My mum had great powers of persuasion with my dad, who afterwards said I was worth it! My faith in her was rewarded as nothing more was said about the price – I don't know how she did it! A fitting was arranged, knowing that I would have to watch my weight, the wedding not being for another six months, as allowing bulges to appear would definitely spoil the overall look of my outfit.

I remember, as the time was approaching on my big day, I went into the bathroom to 'put on my face', very calmly applying it and getting everything right. No unsightly bulges had appeared, fitting into my wedding dress easily. I felt beautiful and radiant! Walking up the aisle on my father's arm, feeling like the queen of all she surveys, beaming at everyone. Then I was next to Ian who glanced at me at last, and was rewarded with the biggest brightest smile I could muster. When it was time for the vows my confident 'I will' rang through the church as I made sure everybody could hear. We went into the vestry to sign the registry, a lot of kisses and hugs being in evidence, and today there was no holding back and no shyness in evidence. I was too happy and radiant to bother about any of those stupid inhibitions.

Being at the end of January we were very lucky with the weather as it didn't pour it down while the photos were being taken – a bit blowy and a might chilly but it didn't snow and hail until we were inside. We even got a bit of sunshine somewhere among the festivities!

We had a lovely meal with speeches that I am sorry to admit I can't remember as everything was in a bit of a haze – I must have missed some gems – but I am sure I can be forgiven.

My Wedding

Walking on air

Stars in my eyes

Love in my heart

Hope for the future

Bustle all around me

Calm enfolds me

Tranquillity surrounds me

Love fills my innermost being

Proud father

Leads me down the aisle

Mother, dabbing at her eyes

Both so happy for me

New life

New beginnings

Knowing he is the right man for me

Willing to work

Towards our dreams

At the reception the thing that has stuck in my mind was when one guest, who was really excited for me, pumped my hand up and down so vigorously, that the sherry in my wineglass flew through the air and covered everything in sight!

Ian tried to scotch the more mischievous of our guests by ordering a taxi to take us to the airport where we were staying the night, before taking off to Majorca for our honeymoon; Ian's dad didn't like that idea and let us use his car for the journey so our friends were able to use their creativity in decorating that, so no one was disappointed. As we were living in London decoration of our home-to-be was not possible, so we got off lightly.

We left the reception a bit early as we were tired and wanted to get settled into our room at the airport hotel; so we waved goodbye to the revellers, with old boots and streamers cascading behind us, and lots of cheers and frantic waving of hands. A special hug and kiss for both sets of parents before we went on our merry way.

I don't think either of us understood what marriage was all about and we both got quite a shock when we realised to whom we had committed ourselves. One thing I found very hard was the fact that Ian was not at all romantic and found it difficult to show his feelings. Opposites attract they say! I am also very bossy and try and tell Ian what to do, which doesn't always go down so well, as you can imagine.

As time passes we are learning to compensate for each other. He is opening up and sharing much more and romance has become part of our lives. I am learning not to talk quite so much as I realise he needs some quiet time to himself, also trying not to boss him about too much – often failing miserably – I am not saying it has all been sweetness and light but through our struggles we are coming to an acceptance of one another with maybe a few hiccoughs now and then – after all we are only human.

Our growing together was complicated by the arrival of children. Probably because I only had one brother and I missed company; I decided I wanted four youngsters so that mine would not feel the same way – to the dismay of Ian.

Peter, my brother, was four years older than me and of course was allowed much more freedom, which I resented. He had lots of friends and I didn't have any so I thought it was all rather unfair. I didn't learn from the fact that he was friendly and accepting of others, whereas I was a bit of a prickly pear with a very sensitive ego! I didn't realise that. I was very adept at keeping my blinkers in place. I only saw what I wanted out of life, forgetting that others have different ideas and desires than me. Maybe it might be a good idea to think of their feelings sometimes!

I remember when I was only very young, we used to share a bedroom and Peter gave me a potted history lesson on the Battle of Hastings. I was quite fascinated with his superior knowledge and enjoyed having the fellowship of my brother as I didn't have much company. Thanks are due to him for taking the time to read and give me feedback on my manuscript.

I blamed everybody else for not coming and talking to me without seeming to realise that I needed to make the first move. My lack of people skills frightened others away although I was under the deluded opinion that I was a very friendly person. You would have thought that my lack of friends would have told me something! People thought I was very stand offish, not realising I was painfully shy. This realisation has helped me to respond to someone who, maybe, is feeling the same way, and risk making the first move, often being pleasantly surprised by their reaction.

When I was older I did spend some time with Peter's friends as we all went to the Church Youth Club. They decided to start a badminton club where much to my relief, as I thought I might be too young, I was allowed to play. There was one boy who I had a real crush on and I had all sorts of dreams about him sweeping me off my feet, but of course he was oblivious of me. Imagine my feelings when another young lady appeared on the scene. My heart was broken and I went into a decline – until someone else captured my attention!

With all four of our children the births were all very quick, even when I had to be induced with Carl our eldest. My blood pressure went up quite high and they took me into hospital because they were worried about me. I had put on about three stones in weight as I was always nibbling on sweets to try and get rid of the horrible taste in my mouth that was always with me. By the time Carl was born I was like a little barrel – I am only five feet two so I gave the appearance of a huge football with legs.

In the end they decided to induce me as there was always a danger of toxaemia that can harm both baby and mother. When they put me on the drip it took me till the second bottle to start to go into labour. When I did I was pretty quick and one nurse came rushing in when she heard my moans and said, 'She's ready,' and was rushed into the delivery room with Ian following in hot pursuit.

Maybe this should have warned us about my speed of producing for the future. Ian said it was the most miraculous event he had ever seen. I was too busy pushing to notice anything miraculous about it! The midwife gave me my newborn baby to hold. Then as that feeling of wonder came over me all the pain and anxiety went as we gazed down at him.

I had an awful lot to learn about parenting and I was very keen on the discipline – too much like my dad – and poor Carl did not have a lot of tender loving care. One time I remember, when he was only a baby, he was really crying hysterically. I would not pick him up. Ian's mum and dad were with us and they really got upset with me. Finally Ian picked him up. I was really cross about being over-ruled but looking back, I am really pleased that the care Carl needed was given to him.

Another time, when by then we had two more children, we were on a beach and Carl was wandering off on his own and would not come back, so I walked off and left him, dragging everybody else with me. We walked quite a way until Ian could go on no farther and went back for him. He was in quite a state when Ian found him and brought him to us. Now I can't understand how I could have been so hard and uncaring. It was as though I did not know how to show my love, too frightened to lower my barriers and let even my family see the vulnerable me. Perhaps their love was able to melt the ice that seemed to be round my heart and gradually set me free from myself. Thank you everyone.

Two years later I became pregnant again, everything progressing normally except for the usual heartburn and morning sickness until I neared the time I was due. When my contractions started the midwife was called. After examining me she said I had plenty of time and told me to have a bath. Whilst relaxing in the pleasantly warm water I became rather alarmed as the contractions became stronger and more frequent. I communicated my panic to Ian who hurriedly rang the midwife again. It didn't take me long to get dried and out of the bath as things were getting ever urgent. Having been examined again I was bundled into our car and told if things were getting too imminent to stop, as the midwife was following, and she would come to our rescue.

We finally arrived at the hospital where they transported me in a wheelchair to the labour ward. On the way the young nurse asked me if I wanted to go to the toilet. Whilst there I had the urge to push so realising there was more urgent things to attend to I hurriedly scurried back to the wheelchair telling the nurse what had happened.

There was a panic-stricken expression on her face as we speeded up to the ward. I was helped onto the bed with the little nurse pleading me not to push till the midwife arrived. Just as I couldn't hold off any longer the midwife calmly entered.

Her demeanour rapidly changed as she assessed the situation and just managed to catch Keith as he shot out into the big wide world. I can't remember much after that as I was in a state of shellshock. The nurse on the ward said I had gone through quite a lot so I had to just take it easy. I needed no prompting on that account so I just lay back on my pillows and went to sleep. I awoke to find Ian standing there looking a little like I felt as I think he was in a state of shock too. He gently kissed me and told me to go back to sleep and left me to my slumbers.

I really wanted to breast feed all my children as I felt it was better for them, but with Carl the midwife insisted that he went on the bottle straight away and gave me no advice on breastfeeding at all. Being very inexperienced I just did as I was told.

With Keith I was determined as I had looked more into it and told the midwife of my plans. I persevered but she said I didn't have enough milk and persuaded me to bottle feed him as well, being frightened of me getting sore. I think babies are more with it than we give them credit for so, because it was easier from a bottle, Keith twigged and didn't really suck very hard when I tried to feed him, so I dried up and had to give up.

With my next two I was more successful although I remember being in a state of undress most of the time when they were babies so nothing much got done – the story of my life!

There was quite a lot of rivalry between Carl and Keith especially when Carl was given a pedal police car for his birthday. I tried to teach them how to share but Keith always seemed to be riding in it. I don't think I was a very good mediator, and I think Carl gave up after a bit as it was too much hassle, he was all for a quiet life!

It was two years later that the patter of tiny feet was again on the horizon. Everything went by in a haze as the two other youngsters kept me on my toes and the nine months went by really quickly. The great day quickly arrived and the midwife was speeding me in her car to the hospital with my contractions again getting ever faster. We did manage to get to the delivery room this time and everything went well. Ian just missed the birth by a couple of minutes as he was at work and didn't leave in time. Mark was put in my arms and Ian and me cooed over our handiwork.

After that I had my hands full with three under five, my days being full of dirty nappies, liquidising food and other general caring tasks, I fell into bed exhausted every night. This cured the difficulty I had of getting to sleep. Ever since then I have had no problem on that account just falling unconscious as soon as my head hit the pillow. I am not saying the answer to insomnia is to have four children, as I think that might be going a bit far, although if you want to try it don't blame me if it's more than you bargained for!

This continued for three years when dirty nappies were behind me and things were a bit more on an even keel. I had two at school and I knew I could cope with another baby as I felt my family was incomplete with only three. I was told that with my fourth I shouldn't be quite so quick. Secure in that knowledge the pregnancy progressed although I decided not to take iron tablets as I thought that's what caused my sickness with my earlier pregnancies. This meant that I was very tired all the time but at least I was able to keep my food down.

The time was drawing near but I thought I still had another week to go. That weekend I was most uncomfortable and felt something was going to happen soon. Ian's mum and dad came over from Saddleworth to see us, and mum said that something would happen soon. I could not keep still and was wandering about like a lost soul.

Ian had a long way to travel the next day so off he went leaving me still feeling as though I had ants in my pants! As the day progressed I couldn't get rid of that expectant knowledge of something not being quite right. I eventually rang the midwife. She said she was not due on yet but asked me if I could wait for another hour. I said I thought so and returned to my bed.

She came sooner than she intended but when she examined me her laid back attitude transformed into a rather panic-stricken urgency. She tried ringing the ambulance but no joy so once again I was loaded into a car that sped down to the maternity hospital. The midwife told me that she had given her trainee time off – no babies were due on that day so she was on her own.

She requested my patience till she could get some help from other wards. We just managed to get to the delivery ward when the baby started arriving and I was soon holding her in my arms. I was left on my own for quite a long time but I did not mind that as I gazed into the face of my only girl. It was nice to have another female in the family!

As we were not expecting a little girl we had no names ready. I wanted to call her Alanah but Ian would have none of it so we finally settled on Karen Mary. Ian told me that he broke all speed records when work managed to get in touch with him to warn him of the imminent birth. He finally arrived looking breathless but happy as I showed off our new arrival. We marvelled at having a girl!

We both decided that I should stay longer in hospital as the thought of dealing with our three youngsters as well as a newborn baby was more than I could cope with at present. Ian took some time off work but the plans soon changed as a couple of days later, when he came to visit with the tribe, he begged me to come home as they were all missing me; Keith especially being rather naughty. It's nice to feel wanted so I didn't really mind, although there was a little bit of regret as I packed my bags and waved farewell to everyone.

There was the usual trauma as all four were growing up. One time I remember frantic phone calls from the junior school when Carl nearly knocked his front teeth out – twice in the same week! He has beautiful teeth now with the help of the orthodontist, where he had to go for a course of treatment with those horrible braces being the order of the day.

Mark was about the same age – about nine or ten – when I got home to find him at the next door neighbour's, with a really nasty splinter in his leg, from a slide in the local park. It had wooden sides that were not supposed to be used for sliding down, but Mark thought it a good idea at the time! He ended up with a very long splinter embedded in his leg. I took him to the doctor who sent him down to the hospital. They had a great deal of difficulty getting it out, finally taking two operations. We were going on holiday to France two days later and he had to have the stitches taken out there!

Keith was much older when Ian had to rush him down to hospital. He had been out with his mates on their bikes and they were going cross-country. Apparently his friend went down this very steep slope quite safely, so of course Keith followed, ending up going head over heels and gashing his face, near his eye, on a rock. Due to some very skilful needlework by one of the nurses they managed to save his sight, so we have no complaints about the National Health Service, as they have always come up trumps for us.

Karen was a very adventurous young lady, many a time when she was a baby I would find her balancing precariously on the top of our kitchen wall units, when I had left the kitchen steps too near. She only ended up in hospital when she had been celebrating the finishing of senior school with her friends, finding herself flying through the air when a car knocked her down. There was no permanent damage although she was very shaken up and had some very nasty bruising!

Kids

Toothless smiles

Gurgles of joy

Cuddles

Sloppy kisses

Worth

All the struggles

All the work

Send you scatty,

Drive you wild,

Little knees bruised

Little fingers cut

Screams of agony

Tears flow

Furrowed brows

Off to school

Frantic rush

To get there on time

Hungry baby

Whimpering in pram

Reluctant schoolboy

Drags his feet

Growing up

Reaching for independence

Becoming

Their own people

Maturity dawns

Young men working

Young woman studying

Where have the years gone?

Joy breaking forth

With gratitude

For all they have become

Knowing

They will go the extra mile

Striving for excellence

I would like to thank Ian and our young people (mustn't call them kids now!) for all their understanding and patience that has been shown me in my struggles to support and care for them. I apologise for the many mistakes I have made and ask you to believe that I did the best I could, being the person I was, and ask your forgiveness for any hurt I inflicted on you. I love you so much and am really proud of the people you have become. It really does give me a belief in the strength of the human soul and the ability of children to overcome the difficulties we as parents give them. Thanks are also due to Ian for meticulously going through my manuscript, for dotting all the eyes and crossing the tees. It is wonderful to have someone with the gift for detail that has certainly been left off my list of attributes!

The power of the human mind is much stronger than most people realise and I really do believe, although I might be wrong, I often am, that my own thoughts can control my environment. As I have become more positive I have become happier in my outlook and that has released the love that has lain dormant within me for so long. The barriers are coming down now although I still allow them to creep back up sometimes, especially when I feel threatened. Even when I feel down, I know it is up to me. I have to give myself a good dose of positive thoughts and not let my naturally negative mindset win. Being positive will always be triumphant so long as I never give up trying and believe I can do it.

Happiness is something for which I have always been searching. I know now, for me, that it is a decision and I am in control of my own feelings. I have to be careful not to bury hurts that need to be addressed but if I act happy even though I feel depressed, my mind just can't take it; I have to cheer up, especially if I smile a lot. I have read somewhere that smiles release chemicals called endomorphins that boost our immune systems and make us feel great. I have tested this idea and I really am sold on it. It is surprising what a smile can do! Any chance of you trying it? It won't cost you a penny, although it might give you a few more wrinkles if it becomes a habit, but who cares if it changes your life for the better!

CHAPTER 7

Challenges

My mum said I had a succession of boyfriends before Jim and Ian. These boys never lasted very long and every week I would bring someone different to be vetted by my parents. That was one thing they were very strict on. I had to bring my current boy to the family home for tea. It must have been quite nerve wracking for them and some were so short-lived that it never got that far, which I think was rather a good job in some cases! They had to be really keen to allow themselves to be subjected to such torture.

There was one boy who I met at another youth club. He asked me out and we arranged to meet at the town hall. He was very tall with black hair and I definitely rather fancied him. Imagine my feelings when he did not turn up. I felt as though I was going to blow up until another boy started talking to me, who had also been let down, I began to feel a bit better. That soon changed when he took me up a back street and started coming on a bit strong. He apparently was a disc jockey on Radio Caroline so that put me off disc jockeys for life. I quickly beat a hasty retreat and caught the bus home. When I next saw my date he made all sort of excuses, but I was not impressed and that was the end of a beautiful friendship.

Ian and I never really talked about having children but I always felt there was something missing until we finally had a family of four. Ian didn't have much option because once I make my mind up it is not an easy task to change it. Part of the challenges could be that Ian is as obstinate as me so if we both decide on opposite ideas we have to come to some compromise. It all seems to work out as Ian has a knack of finding a way round it so that we are both happy. If there was a deadlock I did sometimes back down seeing as the Bible says the man is the head of household, although I must admit I found that difficult.

Ian then got another position that took him away from home a lot. Although we did not like it, it did me a lot of good. With Ian away I had to be more independent, my support having been taken away.

Again this caused a few challenges, as Ian had to get used to me being more confident. I even asked that we could have a joint bank account as I had no way of getting money when he was not there. He agreed, which made me feel a bit more in control. Me being me I could quite easily forget to ask for the money I needed which would have filled me with panic if that had ever happened. In fact it nearly did once which made me realise the precarious position I had let myself be put in.

I sometimes seem to have a missing link in my thinking where I don't always see the obvious. For example: when a friend goes on holiday and I ring their phone number expecting a reply. It's not that I have just forgotten it's as though I don't understand that when someone is on holiday they are not at home. It is difficult to explain and I sometimes get very strange looks, when my conversation gives the impression I have not been listening to what has been said!

Whilst he was away I spent most of my time looking after babies and young children as our family increased. At the earliest opportunity I was off out, youngsters in tow, pestering the life out of other young mothers who really wanted to get their work done. I did not see this; I thought I was bringing sweetness and light into their lives, just descending on them without as much as a by your leave.

Housework was left undone. If I could have only faced up to what had to be done and do it with a smile on my face I would have felt much better about myself. This is still a challenge; my aversion to housework has not changed over the years. When I remember to tell myself that the sooner it gets done the sooner I can go on to more pleasant pastimes, the incentive returns and I start with a will and it is soon finished.

Ian was on sales ten years but the pressures began to build up on him and he wanted to see more of the family, so we decided to start our own company. He would become a contractor and use agents to find work. We were both directors and my task was to do the books.

Unfortunately figures and me are not on the best of terms so I really struggled. In the usual male way Ian just left me to get on with it. Every month when the day of reckoning approached I was filled with trepidation. Finally I took the plunge and spent hours sifting through the friendly figures, which for me, often turned into mental monsters. It was not often that they balanced first time so I had to go over them again to find one elementary slip that had made all the difference. I knew when that dreaded day arrived nothing much else would get done. What really frustrated me was that Ian would have dashed it off in a couple of minutes with no problem at all.

My Friendly Foes

Numbers!

Taunting me from the page

Laughing at my feeble efforts

To persuade them into submission

Characters

Showing compassion

As I persevere with no hint of surrender

Gaining respect from my adversaries

Finally gaining the victory

With a feeling of gratitude

To the old warriors of the battle

Who have taught me so much

About that time the doctor diagnosed that I was suffering from depression and I finally agreed to take some anti-depressants. After a few months these did the trick, although I did hate the zombie-like feeling they gave me. The following year at exactly the same time (nearly to the day, my doctor said) saw me at the surgery again. When I told the doctor that I did not like the side effects of the last drugs he prescribed a different type. I happily departed with my prescription.

After a few weeks I awoke in the middle of the night feeling the call of nature. I got out of bed and proceeded to collapse on the floor. As the need was getting rather pressing I struggled to my feet and this time got as far as the dressing table where I promptly had another blackout and found myself on the floor again. Dragging myself to my feet I managed to get to the door.

By this time Ian realised something was not quite right and a drugged voice from the bed said, 'What's up?' No answer came the reply as I was focused on one thing – the bathroom. I made my perilous way to the smallest room, collapsing twice on the way. By this time Ian had crawled out of bed and found me on the floor in the bathroom. He helped me up and I had reached my goal. What a relief! He managed to get me back to bed without further mishap. Ian wanted to ring the ambulance – which would have been a good idea – but I said I was feeling better. I had made a mess of my face – looking like I had had a major bout in the boxing ring – I certainly was not with it!

The surgery was closed so I said I would ring the doctor later, as Ian had to go to work. I don't know how the children got to school as the younger two were only at primary, but everyone seemed to rally round, and it was all sorted out. When they had all gone I managed, with a supreme act of will, to get to the phone and rang for the doctor. I also rang the vicar to tell him what had happened. People rallied round and really supported me and it made me realise how lucky we were to have so many supportive friends.

Ian had made me a flask and something to eat so I just relaxed on the pillows on my return to bed. When the doctor arrived he looked rather worried, but he did not have a clue what had caused it, and said he would arrange for me to see a specialist when I had recovered. He told me to just concentrate on getting back to normal and to come and see him when I had recovered.

My speech was slurred and I was not able to think straight or string words together to make any sense. The rest of my convalescence was a blur; all I could do at first was sleep. One of our friends from church came to look after me at lunchtime and all I had to do was sit back and relax. It was never discovered what had caused the blackouts, the doctor blaming depression, although I was convinced it was the last lot of anti-depressants. I was referred to a specialist and he sent me for a test for epilepsy. This did prove to be negative although when I was going through the tests I had a terrifying panic, a spaced-out feeling. They had to stop until I got myself together again. The test entailed a lot of flashing lights that I didn't like but after the first false start I was able to control my reaction. The time soon came when I had to get back to normal life and soldier on!

Depression is such a terrifying illness; the medics don't seem to know what to do except give anti-depressant drugs that have uncomfortable side-effects. I am not saying that they have any choice in the matter, they do the best they can with the information they have.

It has been suggested that hiding from uncomfortable emotions might be a cause. I have been exploring that with counselling but never got anywhere with it. It might have been because I was not ready to delve too deep. It was here, though, that I was told I had a gift for writing. I had showed my counsellor some of my work I had had published in the Day Centre newsletter, so these sessions did move me on. Everything does happen for a reason although sometimes I do find it difficult to see.

I have just started another course of counselling which I am finding much more beneficial. It is very helpful when you are believed that something does not feel right. I always knew that something was holding me back from reaching my full potential. It is exciting to actually do something about that gut feeling. My gratitude goes to the young lady who helped me work through the hurts of the past and gave me the confidence to forge forward to pastures new.

By facing up to my traumas of the past, some I didn't even know about until I started writing this book, has given me peace and acceptance of myself I have never had before. I thought I had gone as far as I could, but as I move on, the difference is tangible – I can almost touch it. My counsellor says she can see a real difference so I know it is not just my imagination. I am nearer to relaxing but I know I'm not quite there, looking forward to more exciting revelations that will move me on ever further!

The psychiatrist referred me to an anxiety management course that really was just what I needed. We did lots of exercises and of course talks, including a story about Glug the caveman, which was all very enlightening.

This taught me how stress is something we all need, for example, if you were crossing the road with no car in sight and suddenly a vehicle appeared round the corner, going at a great rate of knots heading straight for you; you wouldn't have to think about it, adrenalin would be coursing through your veins and you would become the fastest sprint runner in the world to get out of the way.

It is when we have a feeling of panic in a normal situation, like when we are in a crowded place and we make the assumption that the crowds were the reason for the panic. Ever afterwards we avoid crowds like the plague because we reason that that causes us to panic. Adrenalin is for our good, not to cause us difficulties. People being people, we always seem to be able to turn a positive into something that will do us harm.

It made me realise that I was the only one who could get myself out of this downward spiral. If it was to be it was up to me! I had to begin to accept responsibility for my own actions and feelings. I always thought I couldn't control or change them but this course gave me techniques that showed me how. I became quite excited at the new feelings of being in control and I started moving forward knowing I would get there in the end. I am still on that journey and the further I travel the more excited I get as I begin to see my full potential.

There are a lot of misconceptions about feelings controlling how you behave. It was a real eye-opener to be told that it can be the other way round; feelings can be controlled if you really want them to be.

Armed with this knowledge I began to put this idea into practice with something called self-talk, finding that if I told myself I felt great and kept on repeating that, that was how I really felt. It wasn't too long afterwards that I began to see the positive side of the situation and I really did feel fantastic!

Another idea that worked for me was the knowledge that everyone was more interested in their own agendas rather than mine; so that people were not looking at me and criticizing me as they were too concerned with their own issues. That helped me to begin to take myself less seriously and even to laugh at myself sometimes.

It also helped me to realise that to make friends I had to show interest in other people and listen to them, rather than be continually talking to hide my own insecurity and lack of confidence. I was able to give people the benefit of the doubt when they treated me in a disrespectful way, as they could possibly be stressed up about something in their own lives, and their mind was on other things.

This improved my self-image, but because it is hard work to change my way of thinking it is easy to forget and go back to the old way of behaving. It took me a long time to realise and learn these revelations and I had to hear about these ideas again and again before it has finally sunk in – I hope!

It's like riding a horse round a jumping course. I think that hurdle is over and on to the next one, but before I know where I am the same jump is approaching and the lesson is taught once again. So it goes on until the penny finally drops and the next is on the horizon, usually something that stretches me way beyond what I think I can endure!

I was very grateful to the psychiatrist for sending me on that course but I really didn't relate to him and felt just like a number on a file. He just didn't seem to care about me personally and wanted to get onto the next patient as soon as he could. It might be that he was too busy and had so many people to see that he was stressed out of his mind. That didn't help me though.

He put me back on anti-depressants that didn't impress me at all. I decided to make it a goal to gradually get myself off them. I did not like the idea of the same thing happening again, as I blamed the drugs for those blackouts. When I achieved that goal, the next time I went back to see him I informed him of what I had done. He did not seem to be bothered so after seeing him once more he discharged me, much to my relief as I felt we were wasting each other's time.

This period really helped me with self-esteem as I began to take more control of my life but I was still on the wrong track as I kept on doing what I had always been doing – running the house, going to the Day Centre as a member, and pursuing my hobbies (this is not to say these are not worthwhile pastimes.) This is right for some but not for me.

It was when I persuaded my doctor to write a letter of referral to MAPS, Mind Arts Project Stockport, which I had heard about at the Day Centre, when I began to have an inkling of what I could be doing with my life.

I was interviewed and accepted as a suitable student and arranged for my first session with the creative writing group. I really found this was what I wanted to do, but I still did not get the message. I did not write outside the MAPS sessions except for the odd time I worked on my story. It took me years to see the light as I thought my writing would not interest anyone else and I was just doing it for my own self-knowledge and enjoyment. I would like to thank everyone at MAPS, especially Michael and Jacqui for all the support and help they have given me. They have even published a book of my poems, this giving me a taste for seeing my name in print and I have gone on from there!

Then I began to spend a little more time on it and found I got so engrossed in my task that time passed so quickly I wondered where the hours had gone. I felt so much better about myself and was really pleased with some of my efforts. I was still a bit worried that it might just be my imagination, and my hopes were only really pipe dreams that were never going to come true.

In a training system that we have become part of we have been taught that if you really believe in something and are excited about it, never quit and never give up; that is easy to say but it is only winners who can do it so I have to ask myself the question whether I am a winner or not. The answer is <u>If I think I can, I will, and if I think I can't, I won't</u> so it is up to me. One of my favourite sayings is: <u>'I'm a winner, there ain't nobody going to steal my dream!'</u> So guess what I'm going to do? Quitting is not an option if I am really committed to my writing.

It has taken me such a long time to find out what I am meant to be doing. I am even calling myself a writer now. It gives me such a thrill when I have the courage of my convictions.

There is a real purpose to my life and I am really enjoying what I am doing – it's a different sort of feeling – a bubbly sort of effervescent joy that wells up inside me. It doesn't matter if people think I am doing the wrong thing, because I know I am doing what is right for me. I don't care what critics might think.

It's a great feeling of freedom! Even when things are not going well and the words and ideas seem to have deserted me I still soldier on; I know inspiration will return if I am patient. To know that feelings of depression and hopelessness have no need to rule my life is exciting. If the storm clouds start gathering and things are looking grim, I have to find a positive book or tape to lift me up again.

Another technique I have found helpful is to confront those black feelings, say 'Stop' and pull them out into the light. Give them an airing and look at why I think I am feeling that way. One time when I did that, I found I had experienced rejection by people when I was out and about.

I am always talking to anyone who is around and sometimes I get ignored. It might be because they have other things on their mind rather than they are unfriendly people. It is not a rejection of me but just that they are in their own little world or even if they are unfriendly, it's their problem not mine!

Realising this helped me to see that this probably goes back to my feelings as a child and that it is not relevant now. I have no need to feel hurt as it is not personal so I can reject those dark feelings and can continue on my way with peace in my heart. Concentrate on the good things in life not on what is going wrong. I have to believe I am in control even though it does not feel like it.

There is a mistaken belief that talking to yourself is the first stage of madness. I would like to suggest that everyone does it, even though there is no conscious awareness of this fact. If a definite effort is made to monitor what thoughts are going on in my head, I discovered that a lot of them are self-appraisals and criticisms of how I am doing. I discovered that most were in a negative frame of mind.

The idea that we can think in a different way might be a bit scary to some people; or it may even be a revelation to others that want to move on. It may even be a way of turning ourselves round to a happier outlook on life, if we change how we view ourselves by altering the tone of our inward conversations. If concentration on the good areas and conditions of our lives can be achieved, our potential can be really exciting as we move on with the knowledge that we are capable of much more than we thought possible.

Why not try 'I can do it' instead of 'I can't' or 'I'm a winner' rather than 'I'm a loser'. I keep on trying and persevere with changing how I think about myself. I have to give it time and the positive will start working. Only believe and it can work. Ever thought of experimenting yourself? There is no harm in trying but it is up to you!

Change

Trepidation, Fear,

Suppose it doesn't work?

Just stay the same

But at least I tried,

Nothing lost, nothing gained

Suppose it did work?

Release from the drudgery of my life

Excitement of new horizons.

Freedom

Of doing what I want to do!

Dreams fulfilled

Feeling so much better about myself

Stretching

Towards new goals

Never imagined

Is it worth it?

YES

I am doing it.

My full potential

In sight!

CHAPTER 8

More Growing!

As our children were growing up I began to feel I wanted more out of life than housework, so I enrolled for a counselling course as I always thought I was a good listener! It certainly taught me a lot about myself – most of it I didn't really want to know! It did begin to give me more self-respect. I began to accept the person I really was. Resolving to work on the bits I don't like and be happy with the positive bits of me – yes I did find some of those – and love the whole person that is me, warts and all.

One of the exercises involved thinking back to a memory of childhood. As I didn't think I had any, it caused me a bit of a dilemma. We were told to either draw or make a clay model of that memory. As I was pondering on the subject I came up with something I had completely forgotten.

I was on a beach and my dad had made me a dugout boat in the sand. My brother was not allowed in it and I was sitting on the seat in the boat with my arms out-stretched in gay abandon, a big beaming smile on my face, thinking this is all mine! Peter was standing looking in the boat with an envious expression on his face. My dad was sitting in a deck chair nearby.

My tutor pointed out that I hadn't included my mum. After all those years I must have still held resentment against her for not being there to hold me when I was a newborn baby, even though I knew she couldn't do anything about it.

This makes me feel so sad that I had been harbouring this hurt for so long, letting it eat away inside me, causing my mum so much pain by how I treated her. The knowledge that my hurt was healed before she died, so enabling me to show her the love she deserved, is a great joy to me.

Perhaps sharing this realisation might help others to see how harmful harbouring a grudge is to themselves. How releasing it, when forgiveness can finally be given, meaning life can be continued with a lightness of heart and freedom of spirit.

It is a long time ago now but I know the course did me a lot of good. I don't remember having any relationship problems probably because we were open to each other due to the subject matter we were covering.

I do remember having a bit of difficulty with one of the tutors. I felt as though he was undermining me, probably because of my own sensitivity, taking everything so personally and feeling everybody was out to get me. Although why I thought I was so important that I would warrant everybody's attention, I don't know!

People are too bound up with their own concerns to spend time thinking about me! We had a weekend away as a group and I was able to tell him about how I was feeling during that time. It made me feel better about it, after sharing. I have found that if I can talk about whatever is upsetting me, a problem shared is a problem halved. It then has no chance of festering and being pushed down and brooded on, causing difficulties later on.

Maybe healing can take place just by giving the hurt an airing. In the same way a rug can be giving a good beating to get rid of all the dust and dirt that has accumulated over the months and years. Is that why counselling can work sometimes I wonder?

Not like another course I joined called Caring Services (Social Care). A friend told me that the other students apparently found me very aggressive and arrogant. I think that must have been because I was rather intimidated by them as they all seemed so young and confident! A repetition of my school days perhaps? I remember feeling I had to push myself forward to have a look at something or receive a handout as no one would think of me if I didn't.

There was a fear of being left out and missing something I needed to know as sometimes I didn't hear because of co-ordination difficulties. I remember, once, pushing forward to see something and being verbally slapped down, which had the effect of making me go back into my shell. I was afraid to even say anything after that as I thought nobody would be interested. Letting myself be hurt by a chance remark of a stranger shows how vulnerable I still was.

Maybe I still am very sensitive about how people treat me. More work must be needed on how I feel about myself. I think my self worth has a tendency to go up and down like a yoyo. When I am feeling good about myself I have to be careful that the arrogance does not creep back. The least little setback can send me spiralling down to negative feelings about myself again.

Maybe more positive self-talk is needed. It is so easy to forget to monitor what I am saying to myself, the negative mindset soon taking over if I am not on my guard. It seems so hard work but I know that it will be worth it when it can become a habit to think positive, although I must always be aware of my negative tendencies.

The benefits I have gained from my different way of thinking makes me see that there is no gain without pain, so wherever I am, I never stop learning. I know I have to take a break sometimes: to recharge my batteries and stop trying so hard. If I can only relax I would probably reach my goals much faster!

I really made an effort to be friendly but somehow it did not work. I must have had my barriers firmly in place without realising it. I had to relax but I did not know how. The relaxation techniques I was taught at the anxiety management course did not seem to work. I had difficulty controlling certain sets of muscles, because of the brain injury so all they did was frustrate me. I felt very insecure and unhappy.

I no longer blame the other students, as I am now able to accept full responsibility for my own actions, even though I did not realise what I did wrong! This has helped me give people the benefit of the doubt when their behaviour has been less than acceptable. I almost always remember how I felt and sometimes I can empathise but it is so easy to react and blow my top!

Thinking back there was someone to whom I especially found difficulty in relating. We were put together in a listening exercise – an ice breaker – my concentration was still not very good, finding her difficult to understand, so when I reflected back I was not very accurate. This seemed to really annoy her. Funnily enough she was just the same with me. Probably a personality clash there! We didn't care enough about each other to take time to listen and concentrate on what the other was saying. Maybe that is really what counselling is all about: acceptance of the other person, without judging. Giving them the time to talk, so that they can feel the healing power of having a listening ear.

I seemed to have difficulty remembering people from one week to the next, not recognising them even though I might have been talking to them the week before. If I haven't spoken to them there would be no chance! I think it might have something to do with my concentration, so now I am making a definite effort to notice people, not always succeeding, but I have just got to keep persevering and soldiering on. Could this be another reason why I may have difficulty with relationships?

I became terrified of going there (which of course made me worse) but I did manage to finish the course passing with a few distinctions and merits on some modules.

Whereas on the counselling course they said they couldn't set me free on the unsuspecting public, as my tutor said I could do more harm than good! I think these experiences make me aware of a certain amount of aggression in my character. I thought I was being assertive but I must have overstepped the mark.

I have come to realise, with the help of my counsellor, that it is not what I say, but how I say things and what tone of voice I use. There is no brook for argument and I state opinions as though no one could possibly disagree with me, so of course no one does, and it becomes a definite conversation stopper!

About the same time as I was involved in the counselling course I became a volunteer at a Day Centre for people with mental health difficulties. This really did me good and my confidence increased in leaps and bounds, everybody really encouraging me. For three years I felt as though I was really doing some good in the world, but that was soon to change. I was getting too confident. I wrote some pieces for the newsletter and among them I did my arrogant bit again. Thinking about it makes me want to curl up in a ball and never be seen again, but that is not life, I will just have to continue and do my best.

A member of staff with whom I had supervision helped me such a lot with my self-confidence and growth. He was so encouraging and any criticism that was needed was put in such a way that I never felt threatened. I really missed him when he left. We did keep in touch and periodically we meet for a coffee and a chat and put the world to rights. The other members of staff were all very pleasant people but it was not the same.

Two male members and I were having a laugh in the office when things got a little bit out of hand and I felt I was being rather undermined and belittled. One older guy, especially, was being a bit fresh with me. Being a bit big for my boots I copied what I had seen the staff do. I had a quiet word with them.

One lad was fine but the older man took it very hard. I was blamed for making him very ill. The following day I was taken into the office and the organiser gave me a real roasting. In fact she gave me the sack although she wouldn't call it that. I was absolutely devastated – the Day Centre was my life. She said I could come back as a member, that at the time I was not interested in, as I felt too rejected.

This of course is my side of the story. I am sure the management committee had their reasons but I was terribly hurt. It is the old story – all the good I had done being wiped out by one mistake – it took me a long time to come to terms with it.

Let me tell you what I have learned from it. I have become a much stronger person, able to take the knocks of life more in my stride. I have learned I have to think before I act and also ask advice from people in authority. The ability to accept what I can't change and be humble enough to go back to the Day Centre as a member was a very hard thing to do. I realised that I still needed it as it had done so much for me. It was no good being resentful and bitter as this would only do me harm, as I have learnt to my cost. I still wanted the support that was available if only I had the guts to accept it. I still feel hurt about it but

I look on it as a learning experience and have learned to forgive, as I am sure I don't know the full story.

Perhaps too I was going in the wrong direction again. I have come to realise that no one but myself can cope with my own challenges. I have to accept responsibility, I believe, for what happens to me, as I am causing my own problems. I am convinced, although I might be wrong I often am, that my bad attitudes and negative thoughts were a catalyst that ensured I was heading for disaster.

To me that means I had to change my negative mindset and turn myself round to become a permanent (most of the time) optimist with a positive attitude who shares her love of life with everyone and gives some joy to people. That has become my mission statement to give a bit of joy to everyone I meet. This helps me to act cheerfully even when I don't feel like it, which again uplifts my mood and gives me a much happier day.

I am coming to realise that I am a very gullible and loving person that wants to be liked. I have learnt that making mistakes is part of life and those that don't make any, are not going anywhere, but are stuck in their comfort zone. There is nothing wrong in failing at something, it's quitting that is the wrong decision. There is a wealth of knowledge that can be gleaned from the many things I do wrong. It's just the ability to be open to change and learn from the experience, that is the difficult task.

The messages I received from childhood of what a horrible brat I was, sometimes made me retreat into myself to hide the vulnerable person I am. This gives people the impression I am cold and hard. I have to learn to open up and let people see the real me. I have to banish the fear of being hurt, risk it and just be myself. I have to learn that I am the one that allow others to hurt me and that makes me feel in control: <u>no one can rain on my parade</u> unless I let them. To take responsibility for my own actions gives me a freedom and a release to know I am in charge of my own life. I don't always do what I know I should do – after all I am only human – but I am still learning because as I have discovered the hard way I can't always be right – a revelation to me!

As I grow older I begin to look for solutions to my problems instead of just accepting things as they are and feeling bad about it. Challenges are sometimes disguised as opportunities.

The car was parked on the drive. I wanted to go somewhere and Ian was too tired to give me a lift. so public transport had to be the order of the day. Raining with a cold wind whistling round my ears did not make me a very happy bunny! I then decided it was time to start driving lessons again as I had been trying to get through my test for years – ever since we lived down in London. Ian had tried to teach me but as this nearly ended up in divorce, we gave up on that and I got myself a driving instructor.

Twenty years, half a dozen tests and four children later I still had only a provisional license. I decided that this was the right time to try again. A member of staff at the Day Centre had just got through her test. She said she needed the patience of Job and he got her through so I decided to give it a go. I told him all I wanted to do was enjoy my driving, and not worry about the test. I was really nervous and scared after so many failed attempts.

He accepted this and began to work on my confidence. This soon increased, and I really began to enjoy my driving. I did try one test and failed but instead of giving up on me, like my other instructors had, we soldiered on with a will. The next time I really went into it with a different attitude – rather quietly confident with a determination to overcome this mental monster. I was overjoyed when the examiner gave me the go-ahead especially as he had failed me previously.

This was not the end of the story but only the beginning as now I really did learn to drive. Ian arranged for me to be insured for his beloved car. This really did show his true love for me as it was quite a big step for him to trust me with it. It was a big black seven-seater and I really did feel as though I was driving a tank.

My spatial skills were not good so when I tried to park it in Stockport, in a pub car park, I got myself into a lot of difficulty. I think I might have lifted a car or two up in the air as I did my best to find a place to park. I think a few dints might have appeared in our car as well but Ian was very diplomatic and just accepted it.

In desperation, because I was firmly jammed in, I appealed to a man who was on his way back from buying his lunch, to rescue a damsel in distress. He easily extricated me from my predicament and went on his way with my grateful thanks ringing in his ears, his look of exasperation telling all.

My son Mark had just passed his test too so when a little white panda was spotted in a nearby garage we decided to buy it together. He said he would get the insurance as he wanted to build up his no-claims bonus, which proved to be not a good idea, as he did not realise what a liability he was letting himself in for. I must thank him for his patience and forbearance as I eroded away his no-claims bonus. All the people in my life seem to be endowed with a monumental amount of tolerance and understanding and I would like to thank my family for that.

Time passed and I was getting a little more confident. I had also started a job as a carer so I used to go with Mark to work and then drive home to use it in the day.

On my way to Hazel Grove I was pulling out of a very tricky junction near home when I noticed two cars with their indicators on, coming towards me. Reasoning that I would have time to turn right I pulled out. Imagine my surprise when I saw a leather-clad figure sailing through the air over the bonnet of my car. I stopped to see that he was OK and we exchanged details. Another learning experience I think!

The injured man sued Mark's insurance company and I kept getting very nasty letters that I passed straight on to them. It sometimes seems to cause a lot of trouble being honest. It's almost as if I am penalised for being truthful. Maybe it is temptation not to live up to my own values –

taking the easy way out. I refuse to go along that path; I believe that I have to stand up for my own standards. Not doing so would erode the self worth I have worked so hard to find. I have no guilt feelings to cope with now, being happy with my decision to stop, as it would have been my care for people that would have been ignored.

It could have been that the motorcyclist was overtaking the turning cars so of course they were blocking my vision. Am I exonerated from blame do you think?

I was on the way to work, pulling out from the same junction when I had to stop in the middle of the road as it wasn't clear. Somehow my foot slipped off the brake. (Note: always remember to put on hand brake when stopped for any length of time.) I apparently pulled straight in front of the other driver, which ended up with me being shunted into a bollard in the middle of the road, entirely demolishing it in the process. I was looking in the opposite direction watching the other approaching cars when this happened so I was blissfully unaware of the approaching vehicle. I don't think I can be free from blame for this one! To be propelled in a sideways direction towards a traffic bollard was rather a hair-raising experience; sitting in the car having hysterics was the only thing I was capable of doing at the time.

Some kind soul came to my aid and the police and ambulance were called to my assistance. My poor little battered Panda was dragged off the road into a nearby car park to await for the attention it so badly needed. I was quickly examined and allowed to stagger off home. I am glad to say I did have the presence of mind to ring the office to inform them of my mishap which meant panic stations for them as my clients needed another carer to see to their needs.

Everything went well for a while, except for getting a bit too close to a huge artic. I heard a rather unnerving scraping sound as I turned into the junction. I stopped and so did the other driver who was very concerned about me; but when only a slight scrape was noticed on my car he went happily on his way and I continued about my business completely forgetting about the incident.

I somehow managed to go through life-threatening experiences and just walk away from them not giving a thought of what may have been the consequences, not even offering up a prayer of thanksgiving for my safety. My feeling of gratitude fills my heart with wonder as I realise the gift I have been given without even acknowledging it.

Mark did eventually buy his own car and very generously said I could have the Panda but it didn't last very long. After spending a lot of money on the repairs the clutch packed up. This would mean another hundred pounds so I decided to scrap my little friend.

Happily someone at the garage noticed that there was a tape player in the car and took it out for me. It belonged to Mark so losing that would have really tried his patience even more but, thank the Lord he was not called on to draw on his reserves of goodwill. She was taken away and the garage gave me a pound or some minimal amount for her that left me feeling particularly upset. A learning experience again, to accept things you can't change, but that is a very bitter pill to swallow sometimes!

After this I began to use the family vehicle again although I was back on the bus most of the time as Ian needed the car to get to work. He did eventually find a way to go to work on the train so I took him to the station and collected him at night which gave me the experience I needed, giving me more confidence in my driving. We did change the car eventually as besides looking a little battered because of my adventures it also had a lot of miles on the clock. Something serious was sure to go wrong soon, so we exchanged it for a Golf.

Nothing major happened to that car except that it helped me to improve my spatial skills by a few learning experiences that only caused minor damage. The next car was a lovely red Honda which was the apple of Ian's eye, although I did find it a bit big, I managed to cope with the size as I was getting more experienced by now.

I think my guardian angel must have had a few bruises and dints in her bodywork by this time but she was again called to her duties when I somehow found a diesel slick to skid on.

I was on my way to see my mum in Oldham. I must have just started applying the brakes to turn into the road approaching her home, when the car seemed to take on a mind of its own. It careered off the road demolishing a lamppost on its way – was this becoming a habit I wonder? There wasn't much left of the car as it sort of concertinaed, me being trapped under the steering wheel and knocked unconscious. I remember saying, 'Don't do that. It hurts' when they were trying to extricate me from the wreckage. They took no notice and soon I was on my way to hospital with a suspected broken collarbone. The police said that it was not my fault so that was a relief!

As we were supposed to be going to a party that night, I was picking Ian up at the station. This not being possible, due to these unforeseen circumstances, I made use of that very useful invention, the mobile phone, to let him know of the developments.

He got in touch with my brother, who lived nearby, and two very concerned gentlemen appeared on the scene not long afterwards. They were a bit alarmed when they saw my face as it had taken quite a battering again.

The hospital decided to keep me in overnight because I had been unconscious and they wanted to make sure everything was OK. The following morning I saw the doctor who discharged me. My night had not been a very comfortable one as it was impossible for me to lie on my side. It was too painful. Lying on my back was therefore the order of the day, which I do not usually like to do; it is surprising what can be coped with when there is no choice in the matter. I had to get used to that in all my four pregnancies so it was not too hard to adapt to it again.

The next challenge was to get dressed which usually is not a problem. Being right-handed and having broken my right collarbone it was not a good idea to use my right arm – it hurt. I have a slight left-sided weakness because of the climbing accident so my left arm took on a new lease of life; I had to use it more than usual. Even so it was quite a feat of ingenuity to make myself decent. I'm sure the ladies among my readers can imagine the contortions I had to go through to fasten my bra. The nurses were too busy to offer me assistance and I would have to do it by myself sometime, so why not start as I would have to go on.

I couldn't remember my brother's phone number so I had to ring directory enquiries. Another challenge – how to get the number written down – it was not the most legible of handwriting but I could just about decipher it. I was in no fit state to memorise his number as the night before I could not even remember my own name! Eventually Ian and Peter arrived to pick up the invalid; it was decided to go and see my mum to reassure her, as being a mum myself I know how we worry.

Everything went well after that, albeit a bit painful. I went to the hospital to make sure everything was fine and got another appointment in a fortnight, although they wanted to make it a month, but I was not at all happy about that. All they do these days is to let it heal naturally. This made me feel very helpless because I still like to feel in control, so I was most dissatisfied with the situation I found myself in.

There was nothing left to do now but to get on with my life and stop whinging about circumstances. One good result was that I was unable to do any housework. Of course that was no hardship to me, although they did tell me at the hospital I had to move my arm as much as I could, but not to lift any heavy weights, keeping the sling on till the next visit.

Why I wonder do I have the impression that someone is trying to teach me the virtue of patience again? I've been at this fence before haven't I?

I was back at the hospital before schedule as I was in a lot of pain and I was rather worried about it. The specialist very patiently explained that that is what happened with a fractured collar-bone and that I would always have an unsightly bump at the site of the break. He did his best to be sympathetic, but he must have seen so many and heard the same complaints so many times. I was grateful he was up front with me and totally honest, preparing me for the long haul ahead, fighting my way back to recovery.

I am a real coward with pain so trying to practice what I preached – being positive – was a very hard pill to swallow. I don't think I was a very good example of that philosophy with not a lot of smiles in evidence. I think I was able to laugh at myself sometimes with the groans that were wrung out of me when I forgot about my predicament slipping back into the old way of doing things.

Me being me I was soon out and about again, being really astounded by the kindness of people on the bus and in the supermarket when they saw I was having difficulty with some simple task. They came to my aid with such a generosity of spirit that I can't believe the world is all bad as the prophets of gloom and doom keep telling us. There is so much good in the world that doesn't make the national papers. The good deeds of charity raising by youngsters which appear in the local papers and the bravery of young people in helping animals in distress.

Some of the older generation are always calling the youth of today because they just hang about the streets and make a bit of noise. They say they are up to no good, but if there is nothing for them to do they are just keeping company with their friends. Perhaps it is up to us adults to make some provision for their entertainment, maybe even ask them what they want. I know the cry would be 'We made our own entertainment, why can't they?' It is a different environment now that maybe we adults are responsible for, so things change and so, perhaps, must we.

I was very pleased that this is what happened in our village of High Lane when a skateboard ramp was erected in the park because that is what was wanted. It is quite a congregation point now and when the younger ones are just using it as a slide the older ones are happy enough to wait until the children are taken home and they can get on with the important task of perfecting their skills.

The doctors said everything was going well and there were no problems, not for them maybe, so they discharged me and said if I was worried about anything to phone and make another appointment. Off I went feeling relieved that the long delays in hospital were over but still rather sore and uncomfortable.

Life is like that, things go jogging along with troughs and valleys, I have to guard against getting too complacent, too happy with where I am, forgetting about my dreams. I am comfortable but not content as I know there is so much more ahead for me, to reach my full potential. It is so easy to just wallow in apathy, not do to anything. It is too much bother to get off my backside.

Many people are content with just sitting in front of the TV, groaning about life, not wanting to do anything about it. There is nothing wrong in that if that is what they are wanting, but I'm greedy, I expect more! Staying as I am would mean just following the crowd, not moving on; being average. How I hate that word, it means mediocrity to me, with no sparkle in my eyes. Nothing to live for except maybe the next holiday. People spend more time planning their holidays than their life. That is perfectly acceptable if they are happy with where they are but I want more out of my life than that.

My dream is to have the time and the money to do what I want when I want with no worries. I long to be free to help others fulfil their dreams, to have all they desire so that they in turn are free to help others to reach their full potential. I know the only way to be successful is to help others – by giving you receive, that is a fundamental rule of life.

Some people blame God for all the bad in the world but don't you think that is all to do with cause and effect? If man destroys his heritage, cutting down trees, putting pollutants into the atmosphere, the results are unknown as they go against the laws of nature. We do not know what will happen. We have to take responsibility for our own actions, don't you think?

The more I give of myself the happier I become. The more I hang onto things the more I seem to lose, whether it be possessions or spiritual well-being. The gift of generosity is something I am continually working to achieve. It can be such a blessing to others. The selfless giving, for no thought of myself, is something I am striving to attain but my troublesome ego always gets in the way.

Discontent

Nothing terribly wrong
Nothing terribly right
Mild disquiet about life.
So much to be thankful for
So little to moan about
Concentrating on what
I haven't got.
Where is the gratitude
That fills my soul?
Why has it flown away
To far off lands.
What is the answer?

Believing things will change
But knowing
That it is my actions
That hold the key.

I have to do something.
Deep within my heart
I know what needs to be done
I know if it's to be it's up to me
I am responsible
For my own destiny
I need incentive –
To be pulled by my dreams
To do what needs to be done
To fly like a bird again

I feel my own destiny is to give people another way of living; of sharing ways to gain security; of earning as much or as little cash as they want; of not having to rely on the job to be able to buy what they need and want; of gaining control of their lives; of growing to be people they are meant to be; of reaching their full potential. The only way to be successful is by helping others to be successful, learning to listen to people so that a way can be shown to meet their need. I have to stop concentrating on myself. I have to be able to love myself to gain the joy of thinking of others and their needs. Having glimpses of the ability to do this gives me an indescribable feeling of pure freedom as others begin to see their true potential.

Finding the way to reach my dreams has been a journey of discovery for me. To even find out what they are was quite a challenge. I had buried them because I could see no way of ever having them. I have to learn to scrap my inhibitions, to think about the solutions not the problems. There are often opportunities that are hidden under hard work. I have always got to be aware of the possibilities of each situation. Lateral thinking is something I never understood but Ian has shown me how it works – to look at something in a way that is very logical but not the usual, average answer. If it doesn't work the expected way try another angle.

Going the extra mile, that is doing more than is needed or expected, is also another way of ensuring success in my life as others are impressed if the service they receive is better than the average. Striving for excellence gives me a 'feel good' factor about myself that increases my own self worth and makes me feel that I am doing something worthwhile.

The one most important event that has happened in our lives was what looked to be a very low-key meeting with a friend. He came over to our house to show us an opportunity that has changed our lives. At first we did not see the possibilities but as we began to use the training system of books, tapes, functions and advice from our friends who are helping us, our whole attitude to life has slowly taken on a new meaning. We are beginning to see the true potential of what we have got our hands on. It is not for everyone but the more we learn the more excited we get. It is as though the light is slowly dawning in the same way as the rising of the sun when the dawn is breaking. Each moment brings forth a new more brilliant shade of colour that has not been apparent before. We are learning to work together as a couple and although there have been some very high level discussions, tempers are getting less frayed as we are learning to compensate for each other, something which we have never done before.

We are now looking forward to a new life with less stress and the peace of mind that everyone deserves. All that needs to be done is to take action and to keep the belief that we can do it! Good self-talk has now got to be in evidence and we are grabbing hold of this opportunity and running with it.

SEE YOU AT THE TOP!

The Future

What can it hold?

Dreams fulfilled or

Regret filling my heart.

Choices!

Pulled by my dreams

Held back by my fears

Spirit flowing free

Tapping into the pool of knowledge

That is waiting to be used.

Apprehension!

Fear – an imagined monster

That seems so real.

Lay it to rest,

Demand submission.

Action is the key

Change

My thoughts

Look at the positive

Discard the negative.

Dark ominous clouds

That smother

My potential

Let the sun burst through

With joy in my heart.

Action is winning

Inertia is oblivion

Fear has won

NEVER

My heart is calling

I know what is to be done

Just do it

Go for it

I can reach my dreams

They are there waiting for me

Spurring me on

To new horizons

I just have to believe.

Replace the clouds of despair

With stars of hope

THE END

or is it just the beginning?